Fun Times in Boats, Blocks, & Business

"It's been a hoot!"

A Memoir by

Olaf Harken

Cover design, art, and composition of *Slingshot* by Heidi Harken. Photo compliments of Gougeon Brothers, Inc. More information on *Slingshot* in chapter 8, page 150.

Editing done by Heidi Harken, Hilary Harken, Kim Wilson.

Special thanks to Ruth Harken, Wendy Vertz, Cathy Schnitzler, and Kathy Weishample.

Library of Congress Cataloging-in-Publication Data Available

ISBN 978-0996285001

Printed in the USA

Copyright © 2015 by Olaf Harken

To Ruth, Heather, Heidi, and Hilary

Table of Contents

Introduction

After writing this manuscript it occurred to me that it may be my only literary piece. There were a lot of people and stories that I would have liked to write about — my family in particular and other people that make me laugh and have been important to me.

I am blessed with a wonderful family. My beautiful wife, Ruth, is an artist, musician, philanthropist, and mother extraordinaire to our three children. Heather is a math teacher at Carroll University; she and her husband, Neil Evans, have two wonderful girls, Savannah and McKinley. Heidi is a designer, has lived around the world, and now is a mother to a beautiful little girl named Zoey. Hilary is a copywriter, website builder, and lives in California. All three of my daughters have been very involved in the company and also have a love for the water and boating. My three grandchildren are close by in Pewaukee. My family has been supportive to me over the years. I've been able to give my family great experiences traveling around the world — they continue to travel and will have stories of their own to tell someday.

I like to surround myself with funny people — people who make me laugh. Laughter is a gift that some people share abundantly and infectiously. I have been fortunate to be surrounded by many great people who have a never-ending supply of jokes, pranks, wit, and who do hilarious things.

Charlie Miller is one of the best. No matter what the occasion is, he turns it into a joke or performs a prank, and never stops being funny. There are an endless number of stories, whether he's passing people dog bones on hors d'oeuvres plates, clocking his superior in the air force, or hopping in my wife's car before she knew him and running her around on the ice lake in her Thunderbird. I will never forgive him for waking me up with Esmerelda the vacuum cleaner after a wild night at a regatta by turning it on and running it up my chest. He laughs the loudest and longest at his own jokes, which are usually risqué in nature, and tends to repeat them. But even after hearing them many times, I still find them funny. He keeps his sense of humor even in difficult times. He has been a close friend for the past 50 years. We've shared buildings for our businesses, and he's always been involved with us, whether he's giving his opinion or checking in on us.

Dave Rettinger is from San Antonio, Texas and is a lot of fun to be with — he's constantly telling jokes and laughing. He has a great attitude toward life and is always into a new project, accompanied by funny stories. He gets himself into the most outrageous adventures, such as his well-known incident of the blue peanuts, tamale factories, and stinky shoes. With some unique salesmanship, he conned us into the shoe business by "accidentally" dropping a shoe with a competitor's name on it — so we thought if we didn't do shoes with him, our competitor would beat us to it. We only worked together a short time, but we have remained friends for the last 30 years following our introduction through the stinky shoe business.

Dan Schwabe has become a close friend over the last decade and lives somewhat close by. He always has a smile on his face and loves to tease people. He frequently interjects funny comments, and is just a happy person who is always up for anything. He and I drove through Italy with our wives and adopted the nicknames of Frick and Frack after Click and Clack from the auto radio show. When we go out to eat, he'll let the server select his order, and it's always fun to watch their reactions. If invited to a costume party, he shows up with the most authentic costumes and is brave enough to try and jump fully into anything they suggest — he always has a great attitude. One time, he hung onto the rail of a boat as it was pulling away, unable to get on, and unable to let go in time. He was quietly muttering "Help!" before having to commit to falling in the water when they couldn't pull him up. He just makes everything fun because he's such a happy person, regardless of the situation.

Andy Ash-Vie of Harken UK keeps people in stitches with a never-ending supply of narratives and raw jokes. Whenever we see Andy and ask how he is, he quips, "Still short, fat, and ugly." With Andy around, it will never be boring.

"How do you know who is the deceased at a Finnish funeral? He's the only one not drinking." — That's typical Jukka humor. Jukka Herrala, our Finnish distributor, always has funny stories or jokes to tell and he can usually be found with Peter at the hotel bar at 2 a.m. when we are at a boat show. Peter, Jukka, and Göran Rutergson are a real cocktail when together. Göran is one of our good friends, even though we are minor competitors. The three of them snowmobiled across Finland and had a raucous good time.

The first time I remember meeting Frank Betz, we were barreling down the ramp of a multistory parking building next to the Annapolis Boat Show. As we got near the pay booth, he did not even slow down and blasted through the gates, splintering them into pieces. He casually leaned back and introduced himself to Peter and me. He reminded us that we had met before when I rejected his request for a dealership of our Vanguard line of boats, including the FJ, 420, and 470. In spite of our rude response, we became the best of friends.

Frank has a knack for being in the right place at the right time. He managed to get involved in moving the America's Cup. The Cup was flown in from the San Diego Yacht Club, where it was being kept after the famous Dennis Conner had won it back from Australia. The deed of the Cup has very specific handling rules. During transport, it is kept in a beautiful and very expensive case, and is accompanied by an armed guard. He picked them up at the Philadelphia airport and drove them to the Sail Expo show in Atlantic City. Although it was not a customary or fancy way to transport the famous trophy, it was probably safer since no one would have expected it to arrive with Frank in his van.

Frank sailed hundreds of miles with me on *Procyon* and lives in Florida. He spends much of his time playing with his two dogs and sending emails and jokes to the dozens of fans he has in the sailing and financial worlds.

Randy West was the former captain of *Procyon*, an experimental sailboat project I ran (see chapter 8). He can copy just about any accent and has a never-ending supply of jokes about the West Indies. He would always have a pretty girl as a first mate on *Procyon*. When he would get to port, one would be getting on while the other was walking down the dock. He always had funny stories from his adventures. As good a captain as he was, he was always lighthearted and kept the humor going. He eventually wrote a book of his own about some of his adventures.

* * *

My wife, Ruth, and our kids and grandkids have been the center of my life for most of the last forty years, so this is their story also. They were there during the years we made our sailing equipment, and it was their love and support that made our successes and failures worthwhile.

Ruth and Olaf

Hilary, Heidi, and Heather at the Harken 40th Anniversary, 2007

Preface

Reaching for the America's Cup

It all started in a bar, as usual. It must have been 1976, when the Southern Ocean Racing Conference was in its heyday, that my brother Peter found himself at the sailors' hangout in the Avalon Hotel bar in Miami Beach. As one of the major regattas in sailing, the SORC attracted the top teams from all over the world. Peter overheard a group of sailors speaking Swedish at the other end of the bar, and since our mother was born in Sweden, he began a conversation with them. Among the group was award-winning sailor and designer Pelle Petterson, as well as Göran Rutgerson, a sailor and equipment guru who could make and fix just about anything.

Pelle and Göran talked of going skiing in Colorado after the regatta. Peter was an expert on the subject, since he had gone ski-bumming for most of a year instead of going to school. "Jesus, I was such a screw-off," Peter says now, recalling his college days. And at the time our father agreed: that phone call to Pop half a world away — "I've quit the swim team and lost the scholarship, but the good news is that I'm driving to Colorado to learn about how to be a really good skier" — was the end of my brother's financial support for several semesters until he returned to school and brought his grades back up. But here in Miami, nearly 20 years later, the life of a ski bum was about to pay off. After a few beers, Peter agreed to join Pelle and Göran in Colorado. Sure enough, they all had a great time and made some lasting friendships. In fact, to this day Peter and Göran are very close, even though our companies are competitors.

Swedish America's Cup entry, Sverige, *1977, equipped with Harken ball bearings.*

In 1976 our own company had just developed a range of heavy-duty big-boat blocks utilizing Torlon®, a supermaterial made by Amoco® Chemical Company. Bill Lawson, a sailor and engineer friend of ours, had discovered the material working under contract with Amoco®; that discovery launched us into a whole new segment of our business using Torlon® rollers and ball bearings. Our laboratory trials were very exciting, but we still needed to test them on the water, preferably on an America's Cup 12-Meter yacht. Because of Peter's new connection — Pelle Petterson was the skipper of *Sverige*, the Swedish entry for the 1977 America's Cup races — we were able to introduce our blocks into that grand-prix field. After numerous practice races, Pelle commented that our blocks never needed maintenance other than a freshwater cleaning, while their previous blocks had to be taken apart and serviced after each day.

That meeting at the Avalon Hotel bar was the start of Harken's total dominance of all the America's Cup boats for the next 30 years.

* * *

But I'm getting ahead of my story — a story that follows a couple of troublemaking brothers from their Dutch and Swedish origins through the firsthand consequences of World War II and into a childhood in the Philippines, through sports and college and military life, and into a life of skiing, iceboating, and sailing. It's the story of a business built on handshake deals, longstanding friendships, and on a lifetime of sticking our necks out for a never-ending series of experiments — some of which turned to gold, others to dust. Above all, it's a story of what's possible when a couple of screw-offs turn their passions into a profession.

I start with this anecdote about Peter because, while I often use the first-person "I" throughout this book, two other people were present and utterly integral in nearly every episode of this story: my brother Peter and our friend Art Mitchel.

Mitch has been a major player in the Harken company from its beginning. He is a low-key member of Harken, which until 2009 was really managed by Peter, Mitch, and me. Because our family name is the company name, Peter and I get all the hoopla and recognition. But Mitch has spent his career in the trenches keeping us out of real trouble (though, somehow, we still always manage to find some trouble.)

Mitch is a people person, and the employees would often go to him for advice or concerns. Educated at the University of Wisconsin Law School, he served for three years as a lawyer in the Air Force Judge Advocate General Corps at Wurtsmith AFB, a Strategic Air Command base in Oscoda, Michigan. He returned to Wisconsin and worked as a lawyer in the trust department at the Marine Bank in Milwaukee for four years, then at First Wisconsin Trust Company for eight years as vice president for the retirement trust administration. While at the University of Wisconsin at Madison in the early 1960s,

Art Mitchel

Art leaving his last job

he and Peter were roommates for four years and sailed together at the Hoofers Sailing Club. They and two others shared an apartment near the campus. After the military, when Mitch had the bank job, he'd often stop by our grungy little shop to talk about the world he loved, which was sailing; we in turn got his advice on legal and business matters.

One day in 1978 he came by and said he was tired of wearing a suit and asked if he could work for us. He said if there was ever the slightest problem he would leave immediately. Since then, Mitch has been a manager, confidant, and friend. Like Peter and me, Mitch has "retired" but still manages to come in several hours each day.

And Peter: What can I say?

From the time we could walk, we fought each other constantly. I, however, got the short end of the stick, since he was two years older and bigger. He would throw me down and pound away on my shoulder with the knuckles of his hand at the same spot until it was all black and blue. In one fight I managed to grab his hand and hit a desk with his fingernail, tearing it up. Mom took him to the hospital where they cut most of it off. I could hear him scream and was delighted. At our house in the Philippines, my room was rigged with pulleys and a motor from my Erector Set directing a line attached to a locking door latch. There was a creak on an area of the floor he had to walk across. As soon as I heard it, I would turn on a switch, and the motor would pull the line and close the latch. It worked pretty well, but he still beat me up whenever there was a good opportunity.

On Christmas Eve of 1967 in Madison, Wisconsin, I was spending Christmas with Peter in his grubby little apartment, since our parents were in the

Peter in the '70s

Philippines. I proudly gave him his gift of four hubcaps that fit his old Chevy. I had scoured the area junkyards to find them. I wrapped them in newspaper and presented them to him. Instead of saying thanks, he hit me and started a major battle that lasted at least a half hour. By now I was finally a little bigger than him, and we really started to hurt each other. During a break we thought it would be a good idea to stop the fight and went to one of the only open bars and got drunk, which was a lot less painful.

Olaf, 1970

After the Christmas Eve fight we never had another physical fight. In our business partnership and our personal lives, we've had very few disagreements, which was partially due to a simple set of rules we agreed on. If the subject involved products, manufacturing, design, and engineering, Peter would have the final word. If it involved marketing, finances, and administrative operations, I would have the final say. There was just one major exception to this rule: if the disagreement was very serious and involved people, Peter — in his role as president of the company — would make the final decision and take the final responsibility. This system has worked successfully for nearly five decades.

Ironically, we had switched roles since I had a degree in industrial engineering and Peter had a degree in international business. Peter had a lot of knowledge in manufacturing and gravitated towards product development, while I was more organized to write business proposals, create marketing strategies, and handle finances.

The "Blockroom" from the early '80s

Linda Otzelberger with the original Harken shoes, 1987

Peter and I are extremely proud to be Americans — every year we celebrate Flag Day with our employees and a traditional shot of cognac

Tom Frentzel, our partner in furling manufacturing, 1986

Tim Poremba posing as a rich sheikh during the Annapolis Boat Show at the Harken "Shoe Oasis"

Early Harken traditions included beating the cold weather with our in-house band, a pie in the face on birthdays when Charlie MIller was around, a bucket of water over the head on anyone's last day of work, and if anyone showed up with a tie, cutting it off with scissors

Olaf and Peter Harken

Schooner Havana Packet, *sailed by 19-year-old Captain Alke Harken between Cuba and Holland.*

Pop at the helm of a friend's boat

Chapter One

Ship Captains and Engineers: The Harken Family Roots (1778–1945)

OUR FAMILY

I know very little about the early years of my parents. I know even less about my grandparents — one of the reasons I am writing this tale. I'd like my children to know a little bit more about their parents than I know about mine. So this is my story as I remember it.

My father, Johannes Theodore Harken, was born in Hilversum, Holland, on October 23, 1903. His father was a sea captain, and our great-grandfather was also a captain and owner of at least three sailing ships. We have a beautiful oil painting of the *Havana Packet*, a two-masted schooner. The painting survived the war years with our Aunt Dinah and is now in our home in Pewaukee, Wisconsin; that painting gave us the clues we needed to find out more about our nautical history. To find this information, we first visited the Ships Museum in Amsterdam, where we obtained copies of

Mom and Pop as newlyweds

actual documents from the shipping authorities that kept records of captains, ships' names, the types of vessels, the companies that owned the ships, and the year the ships were commissioned. We could trace back to 1778, the year Harke Oelirchs Harken was born near Bremen, Germany. He later moved to Amsterdam. Harke's son, Alke Harken, was the first recorded ship's captain in the Harken family; Alke formed a shipping company called Harken and Company of Amsterdam.

Our father, "Pop," earned a mechanical-engineering degree from the Eindhoven University in Holland. The only story I can remember about his youth was that he built a beautiful model of a steamship that ran on some sort of a chemical engine. He tried it out in The Royal Pond (Hofvijver) in The Hague, and it killed all of the fish in the pond. I also know that my father was a musician and played the violin. I believe he played occasionally with the Amsterdam Philharmonic Orchestra, so he must have been quite accomplished. I think I only heard him play once when I was a child, but I'm not certain of that.

Our mom, Ulla Kjolstad Harken, was born in Malmö, Sweden, on May 9, 1905. Her mother, Alma Kjolstad, was born in Denmark. Alma died when my mother was only 12 years old. Mom attended university in Sweden at the same time as Ingrid Bergman, whom she saw but did not know. I believe Mom studied physical education, and from old photos she looked like she had a happy childhood even though she had lost her mom at such an early age.

Mom in her wedding dress, 1935

Mom and Pop met in Cuba, where Mom was teaching physical education in a school for young ladies. Pop was an engineer in a sugarcane factory. They met at a dance, were soon engaged, and then went back to Sweden, where they were married in Gothenburg in 1935. They moved to the United States, where my father trained with Caterpillar Tractor Company for his new assignment as a representative in the Dutch East Indies. This was in the last decade before Indonesia gained its independence from Holland. My parents lived in Surabaya on the island of Java, where Peter was born on August 18, 1937. They later moved to Medan on the island of Sumatra, near the equator, where I was born on May 6, 1939.

Mom with Peter in Medan, 1938

MY FATHER'S CAPTURE AND OUR ESCAPE

The Japanese attacked Indonesia in 1941 on Monday, December 8, one day after Pearl Harbor. All Dutch civilian men living in Indonesia were inducted into the Dutch army to defend Indonesia.

My father was put into a demolition squad with the mission to destroy anything that could be useful to the Japanese, including the oil refineries, rubber-processing plants, even our own home and cars. The Japanese quickly overwhelmed the Dutch defenders, and my father was captured and spared execution — only because they didn't know he was in a demolition squad. They hated the demo soldiers the most and killed those caught in the act. Instead, Pop was transferred to a prison camp in the jungles of Sumatra. We were told that only one third of the prisoners survived in this camp. My father was one of them. We know very little of his life in the prison camp since he never talked about it except to tell some funny stories. He had a great sense of humor, and even under the horrible conditions he managed to find something to chuckle about, which probably helped keep him alive. He told us about a chicken — the prisoners had spared this bird even though they were starving — who they would get drunk on alcohol they concocted.

In one story, he told of a scam he and a fellow prisoner had which got them favors. They were instructed to translate Dutch engineering manuals into English, which would then be translated into Japanese. They changed the meaning so that anyone trying to follow the instructions from the manuals would end up with disastrous results. They got away with this for quite a few months before they were found out and beaten.

While Pop was imprisoned, Mom, Peter, and I caught one of the last planes to escape and flew to Borneo. I believe we went to the town of Sandakan. From there we somehow got to Wellington, New Zealand. We then moved to Melbourne, Australia, where we stayed for about six months.

In Australia I had the misfortune to visit the local hospital twice. Peter and I were playing in the driveway and hanging on to a car at the house where we stayed. Peter's friends took off without knowing I was hanging on to the rear bumper. Somehow my ear got hooked, and I had to get it operated on.

Peter and Olaf as boys circa 1944

A few weeks later Peter and I had our tonsils taken out. I remember the smell of ether, which permeated the air in the hospitals in those days. I always hated the smell after that; fortunately, it doesn't exist in modern hospitals. It wasn't all bad memories, though: I can still remember the cool delight of the ice cream they gave us to soothe our sore throats.

SS Lurline

From Melbourne we caught a troop ship — a converted ocean liner from the Matson Lines, named the *SS Lurline*. We were in a convoy of ships on our way to San Francisco, and only five of about seventeen ships including ours made it all the way. I was too young to remember, but I think the rest were torpedoed by small Japanese kamikaze submarines. Peter remembers us picking one up with the ship's crane that apparently did not blow up on impact; the two Japanese sailors were dead inside.

We arrived in San Francisco with only a few belongings and the clothes on our backs. Mom spoke nine languages, one of them being perfect English - Peter and I spoke Dutch with our parents, so we had to learn it when we got there. Being little kids, we picked it up quickly. I think it was the Dutch consulate that put us together with a wonderful older Dutch lady we called Tante, meaning "aunt" in Dutch. She lived in a big house next to a grove of redwood trees in Aptos, California. It was a beautiful spot, and actually became a historical landmark. We used to play in the stream behind her house in the redwood grove. Aptos was very close to Santa Cruz and next to the Pacific Ocean, where there was a great

Olaf, Tante, and Pop

beach with big breakers rolling in from the ocean. One day when Peter and I were playing on the beach, we watched an invasion, as U.S. Marines hit the beach with landing craft and armored vehicles in a mock attack. I don't know what invasion they were training for, but it probably was one of the famous Pacific battles.

During the war years we also lived in Palo Alto for a short while, but I remember little of this time. I do remember that the day the war ended we were in Lake Tahoe with friends of my mother's on the beach, and a great cheer went up when we heard the news. Mom had not heard anything about her husband for four years. She didn't know whether he was alive or dead; still, she always kept her chin up and made Peter and me believe everything was okay. She was an exceptionally strong woman, and I don't know how she managed to raise two kids who only spoke Dutch at the time and deal with all of the uncertainties of moving from one place to another, all while holding on to the belief that her Jopi (pronounced YO-pee) was okay and coming home.

The Dutch consulate in San Francisco and the Red Cross found my father, and we were reunited in San Francisco. It was a bit of a shock for Peter and me to see him, since we could only envision him from photos. After being starved in the camp for four years, he was emaciated. But we soon got over that and enjoyed the happiness of having the family back together again.

Pop is reunited with our family after four years in a Japanese prison camp

Chapter Two

Growing Up in the Philippines: Bullfights and Hand Grenades (1946–1957)

THIRD CULTURE KIDS: AN INTERNATIONAL EDUCATION

After the war, we moved to Larchmont, New York, where we lived for three years after our reunion with Pop. Since he'd worked as the representative for the tractor division of Caterpillar Inc., he needed to stop in Peoria, Illinois, for several months of retraining and reacquainting himself with the company. We left Peoria for New York in our little blue Chevrolet named "Bluebird." Unfortunately Bluebird never made it to New York, since we had an accident in Cleveland on our way there. No one was injured badly, fortunately, but we had to take the train to Larchmont, where we stayed in a rented house at 16 Chestnut Avenue. Peter and I went to Chatsworth Avenue Elementary School while Pop worked in the city for Caterpillar.

In Larchmont we had a friend named Jeff who was our first tutor in how to get in trouble. I think Jeff was 12 years old, while Peter and I were 8 and 10. Jeff could talk us into doing anything since he was our hero and role model. He was able to make trouble and never get caught.

Almost.

One day we decided to throw snowballs at passing cars on the Boston Post Road, which was one of the main highways on the East Coast before I-95 and the Interstate Highway System. Our snowballs were hard and icy and packed very tightly so they could be thrown at a long distance. One of the cars passing below had the passenger-side window open. By chance one of the snowballs that we launched went right through the open window and hit the passenger in the ear. The passenger was the wife of a very mean and big man who did not take lightly to the pain that his wife suffered. He came to a screeching halt and chased after us. We ran and ran while this monster chased after us. We made it into town and found three garbage cans in an alley that had just been emptied. We climbed into the cans and hid for probably 15 minutes and finally got out of the cans when we thought it was all clear. Just as we were exiting the alley, a police car came by and motioned for us to come over. The officer took us to the station, where we met with Detective Boyle, who knew Jeff from some of his previous antics. Our punishment was to tell our parents, then go and apologize to the man and his wife. The detective and other policemen in the station joked about what a mean and large man he was, and we were very frightened at the prospect of meeting him face-to-face. We meekly knocked on his door; fortunately, his wife answered and accepted our apologies with a smile and a light scolding. She said her husband wasn't at home at the time and we breathed a great sigh of relief.

Pop got a job offer to represent LeTourneau, an earthmoving-equipment manufacturer, through their agents, the Connell Brothers in Manila. He loved the Far East and wanted to go back even after the prison-camp ordeal. We left New York for Europe on the ocean liner *New Amsterdam* bound for Rotterdam. Peter and I met our relatives in Holland and Sweden as we toured Europe and stayed mainly in hotels.

Once again we got in trouble at the luxurious Grand Hotel Krasnapolsky on Dam Square in Amsterdam. While our parents were out having dinner, we decided to engage in a pillow fight. This was a very nice hotel, and they used real down pillows. Halfway through the fight, the first pillow broke, and shortly after that the second. There were feathers everywhere. The air was filled with them, the floor was covered, the beds were covered, and the room was a disaster. When my parents got over the shock of seeing it, they decided not to tell the management until the next morning. Upon seeing the disaster, the manager requested that we leave the hotel promptly and never return. Needless to say, our parents were not too happy with their little boys.

From Europe we flew to Beirut, Lebanon, where Pop sold equipment to Aramco (Arabian American Oil Company) in Saudi Arabia. We stayed in Beirut for about two months. This was the time before Beirut was a war zone; it was a beautiful city on the Mediterranean and a popular resort area for Europeans and Americans alike. We stayed at the St. Georges Hotel right on the beach while Pop flew back and forth to Arabia. We then left for India, where he had further business to do in Calcutta. This was extreme culture shock. We stayed at the Great Eastern Hotel, and I remember having dinner in the hotel restaurant with about 10 waiters fanning us, handing us our forks and knives, and hovering over us like vultures. On the sidewalks outside of the hotel hundreds of people slept, while cows lay down in the streets holding up traffic but not being bothered since they were holy. Thousands of people were bathing in the Ganges River in almost raw sewage. The heat was oppressive, and it felt like we were in a sea of humanity. It was the worst place I've ever been.

AT HOME IN MANILA

The trip to Manila from Calcutta went through Singapore on a BOAC (British Overseas Air Carrier) DC-4 airplane. The DC-4 was a four-engine plane that was one of the long-distance carriers of the time. In those days planes did not have the equipment to fly by IFR, so flying at night without radar during the monsoon season could get really exciting. Somewhere over Bangladesh we ran straight into a huge weather system, and the plane dropped thousands of feet in seconds. At that time there were actual sleeper berths for first class, and Peter and I were in our bunks. Pop was below us, and the stewardess was carrying a tray of tea. When the plane dropped we were plastered to the overhead, the tea went flying around the cabin, Pop got a good bump on his head, and the plane was in shambles. A huge sigh came when the updraft shot us up, and we bounced and shook our way out of the storm.

"I say," said the captain in typical British form when we landed, "a bit of a bumpy ride now, wasn't that."

Later trips to Manila were on the Pan Am Clipper, DC-6, Lockheed Super Constellation, and the Boeing 377 Stratocruiser, all before the jet age, which started with the DC-7. The big difference between those days and today was the comfort and care, even if the flights took twice as long.

We arrived in Manila — one of the most devastated cities in the Second World War — in the fall of 1949. We could see the massive destruction the bombings had wrought, even though it was four years after the war had ended. Many buildings had collapsed, and the others showed the signs of bullet holes and pockmarks on their exteriors. Electricity, water, and sewage were still under repair. Rats infested the city, and poison was put in the sewers to kill them. Every evening trucks ran through the streets spraying DDT to kill malaria-carrying mosquitoes.

The enigma was that Manila was called the Pearl of the Orient. To the Harken family it really was, since we had just left Calcutta, one of the hellholes of the world. The people we met there were warm, friendly, and fun-loving. Americans had saved them from the Japanese and were not only accepted but genuinely liked. It made the Philippines a nice place to be. The islands were also beautiful in spite of the war damage.

At that time there was a small navy base on Dewey Boulevard on Manila Bay called Seafront, a residential base for the navy personnel in Manila and Naval Station Sangley Point. It was also the location of the American Elementary School. Here's where our longest-lasting friendships began, even though there were just a few of us at the time.

I don't remember much about Seafront except that this is where I started to like girls. My first infatuation was with Cecilia Parrish. Unfortunately Cecilia liked Johnny Baker, who was my next-door neighbor and one of my best friends. Johnny had a bigger house, and I guess he was a handsome little devil. He had a great backyard with a rope tied to a very tall tree that we would swing on. The best method was to ride your bike towards the rope, grab onto it, and let the bike fall over while you went sailing high into the treetops. In my effort to show off to Cecilia, I took my brand-new bike, got back as far as I could to get momentum, and rode as fast as I could toward the line. I grabbed the rope, and the bike went careening off. I went extremely high — until I could no longer hold on to the rope, went sailing through the air, and landed on my back. All I can remember is that everybody was looking down at me and laughing, not realizing that I was hurt. I passed out and cannot remember what happened after that. The only serious damage done was to my ego. I guess I did not impress Cecilia with this very stupid move.

After living in a high-rise apartment, we moved to a new house in a walled-in compound on F. B. Harrison Street. It was called the Chinese Compound, because it was owned by a very rich Chinese businessman. He lived in the great house in the middle of the compound and brushed his teeth on the balcony while making disgusting sounds. There were sixteen houses in the compound with one primary entrance gate that was guarded by Sikhs who had turbans on their heads and carried around bolos, leather thongs with heavy balls on the ends.

They could sling one of these around someone's neck and easily choke them. As a backup they also carried guns. The walls had glass shards cemented into the top — all this to provide a degree of protection against possible thieves, even though crime was not a major problem in Manila at the time. Stealing was fair game since it was a rich-poor society.

Our last house was at 33 Joaquin Street in San Lorenzo Village, a suburb of Manila. It was a modern, single-story house in a secured area and one of the fairly new developments that sprang up in the 1950s. We had a typical staff of what were then called servants, later referred to as domestic helpers or employees. Emilio was our houseboy who later became an assistant to Mom in her travel business after Peter and I left for college. Emilio still works for the travel company forty years later. We had several lavanderas during the years we were there who washed and ironed the clothing and sheets. Our cook was Pedro — he was more than a cook. He ran the household under Mom, and he doted over Peter and me with enthusiasm and a twinkle in his eyes. He was a great cook and well-known in the social circles of Manila. He and Mom created our famous saté peanut sauce, which was originally derived from Indonesia. Our sauce was far superior to the standard Indonesian sauce. Pedro was a strong person, with a mind of his own; he later became a chef in a well-known restaurant after we left the Philippines. Those were happy days, and our house was a nice place to be, with Winky, our Scottish terrier, Dopey my parrot, Mom in her garden, and Pop listening to classical music on his brand-new stereo system.

As kids we frequently wandered the back alleys and streets and felt perfectly safe. We went to the market on Libertad Street — a huge complex of stalls under an acre of tin roofing where you could buy just about everything, from fresh fish to great slabs of meat, black-market appliances, clothing, jewelry, handicrafts, and our favorite: the large and exotic section of snakes, parrots, monkeys, dogs, and tropical fish. We rode our bikes everywhere, took jeepneys into and around the city, and rode the dark green Saulog transit buses that careened through the streets with the conductor hanging out the door, banging on the side of the bus, and hailing for passengers. Usually right behind the Saulog bus was the yellow transit bus racing for the next passenger. It was a Manila that was alive, full of action, corruption, and fun, but was remarkably safe. This was a city that had been beat up badly during the war years and was ready to enjoy life again.

I was 10 years old when we arrived in Manila in 1949 and entered the fifth grade in the American School — the same grade that I had been in at Chatsworth in New York. The main buildings for the American School were located at the intersection of Donada Street and Taft Avenue, which was one of the main streets of Manila. At the corner of the two streets was a typical sari-sari store, a small convenience store found throughout Manila that sells soft drinks, candy, cigarettes, and all of the small necessities of life. This is where we hung out after school. Because of the heat, school began very early in the morning at seven o'clock and ended at noon. There was only one 15-minute recess during the five hours we were in school. We normally had a quick lunch, which we brought from home or bought at the sari-sari store. When we were younger, our parents or our chauffeur would pick us up and take us home. In high school we walked or took jeepneys, which were abandoned WWII Jeeps elaborately painted and converted to carry a dozen passengers.

Because I was on the swimming team from about the seventh grade all the way through my senior year, after school we would walk to Rizal Stadium, which had an Olympic-size pool 50 meters long and eight lanes wide. The stadium had been built for the Asian Games and was only a quarter of a mile from our school. It was a fantastic asset for our swimming team, and swimming was one of the major sports at the American school. Soccer, basketball, volleyball, track and field, softball, and fencing were all offered for both boys and girls. Our strong sports were basketball and swimming, where we often excelled against the other schools in Manila. There were public schools and a lot of Catholic schools in the city that we competed against. The Filipinos loved basketball the most and were very good at it, except that we had a height advantage.

The Swim Team

We had some pretty hot swimmers in the different strokes. Bob Boni excelled in the breaststroke, Fred Elizalde was the 100-meter butterfly champion, and I was pretty good in the backstroke. When I was in Class-A swimming during my freshman year, I won the 100-meter backstroke national championship race. I received a gold medal, which I was very proud of. It looked a little dull, so I decided to polish it up with some Brasso. The gold plating immediately rubbed off, and my beautiful gold medal was now a bronze medal.

One day Peter Nathan, one of our freestylers, left his shorts out in the locker room after going to the pool. We had brought some wintergreen with us just for such an occasion. His shorts were amply doused with wintergreen and left to dry. After practice Peter put on the shorts while his equipment was still a little

American School swim team — Olaf is third from left, top row

bit wet, and he soon started doing a war dance, whooping it up. We really had a good laugh and were very careful to put our shorts in our lockers after the incident.

Our coach was René Amabuyok, who also coached the Philippine Olympic team. We were really lucky to have such a great coach. I remember when he asked the famous Japanese swimmer Furuhashi, who was in the Philippines for the Asian Games, to join us for practice. Furuhashi passed us like we were standing still — he was incredible — but gave us great inspiration to do better.

We had a 10-meter platform for diving, which was really high. Our huge swimming pool looked like a postage stamp from the top of the platform. When we were in Class A, the swim platform was always good for a dare. Just jumping off could be very painful if you didn't point your toes and keep your knees together. When diving, it was pretty important to make a clean entry or you were going to suffer a lot of pain. It was like taking a flat board and being whacked on the back or stomach. Of course we would always give the wrong instructions to a neophyte making his first jump. Keep your feet flat and try to enter with your heels first was a common instruction. The poor sap couldn't walk for a day if he followed our instructions; best of all, he couldn't chase us.

The American School Class of '57

Some of my most enduring friendships are my classmates at the American School in Manila. To this day the class of '57 is still close. More than half of our thirty-one graduates get together several times a year. The bonds that we formed come from being so close and isolated in a small community. We went to school together, we played sports together, and we socialized together, frequently with our parents, who were also part of the small foreign community in Manila. It was a tight-knit group, encompassing every nationality, race, and religion in the city. In the class of '57 we had Chinese, Filipino, American, German, Greek, and Spanish students. We were totally colorblind: a wonderful asset.

A memorable get-together was in San Francisco in June of 2004, where we chartered a sailboat and sailed in the bay out of the San Francisco Yacht Club on the northern shore in the town of Belvedere. There were nine from our class and another ten from classes surrounding the class of '57. We also celebrated our recent or upcoming 65th birthdays.

Ed Schwesinger hosted us and Myra Lowman did the organizing. Myra was a travel agent with a lot of travel experience and had no problem bringing people in from all over. She had a kind heart, and was a tenacious, brave lady. Charlie Clark is our resident physician and psychiatrist. We kid Charlie about his methods of administering to his patients, since he believes there is a drug for just about everything and every ailment: "better living through chemistry." The truth is that Charlie cares about his patients: he ministers to the homeless, drug addicts, and alcoholics in Denver and Boulder, Colorado. He also calls us when he knows that we have a problem and need some support and help.

Myra had been living with cancer on and off for 14 years — Charlie called almost daily to see how she was doing. During a remission, she took my daughter Heidi in while she was working an internship in California. Heidi was able to help her for a while, but then had to move away. She passed away in 2005, but she was not alone. Verney Vines, another classmate, took care of her during the last months of her life. These were the kind of relationships and friendships that we developed back in our days at the American school.

Ed Schwesinger considers the group from the American School as his family, and he constantly shows his concern and generosity toward all of us. He's been a big help to Peter and me as we've worked through the intricacies of a succession plan for our business, donating his time and experience and knowledge pro bono, although we would have gladly paid.

The Polo Club and Yacht Club

In Manila our lives were packed with experiences that were only as lavishly obtainable in the Orient. The glamour of the Polo Club was one example; polo was played there occasionally, but the club was mainly for tennis, nine-pin bowling, swimming, and dining. There was a huge swimming pool and great hamburgers and food. Most of the international community belonged to the club, along with the Manila Yacht Club and the Army and Navy Clubs. Automatic pinsetting machines had not been invented yet, so the pins were set by boys. Instead of trying to knock down the pins, we tried to fire the small balls down the alley at a high speed to set the pins flying and make the pinsetters duck. A perfect split did the best job.

Wrestling with my dad and Peter in the pool was great fun and some of the best memories I have of Pop. Because we were on the swimming team, we also did a lot of laps in the pool and used it for practice some of the time. It was a big club and the center of many of our extracurricular activities.

The Yacht Club was our favorite hangout when we weren't practicing swimming or at the Polo Club. It was located a little more than a mile from school on Dewey Boulevard, named after Admiral Dewey who defeated Spain in the Spanish-American War in the Philippines. The name has been changed today to Rojas Boulevard, for one of the first presidents of the Philippines. This famous boulevard ran along many miles of Manila Bay, and the Yacht Club was right on the bay next to the headquarters of the Philippine navy. The clubhouse was a simple building with a long bar, but most importantly had a large porch overlooking the bay where many of the members stopped to watch the famous sunset over a cocktail. The racing fleets were primarily Dragons and 110s. There was also a fleet of cruiser-racers and cruising boats anchored in the well-protected harbor. The harbor had an enormous breakwater to protect both the navy and the yacht-club boats.

Our first boat *Katsy* was a Snipe and made of wood. We spent hours caulking and varnishing the hull and brightwork.

I raced with Eric Westley on his boat as the third crew in the highly competitive Dragon fleet. Upon returning to the Philippines thirty years later on a business trip, I saw the same Dragons in beautiful condition still in their cradles or tied to moorings in the bay.

Pop had a really unique cruising boat that was quite fast. It was named

Katimka and was modified from a boat that was carried under the fuselage of a B-29 bomber. Made of cold-molded plywood, it was incredibly strong and light. A keel, cabin, interior, and mast with new rigging were added to make it a very nice sailboat with good handling. *Katimka* was about 30 feet long and gave us many years of pleasure cruising.

NO AMOUNT OF TROUBLE WE COULD NOT GET INTO

Manila was heaven for young boys. During the years that we lived there, we managed to create or find trouble everywhere we went, and somehow we managed to survive.

The Grenade Accident

When a war is over, the soldiers do not pick up all of their weapons and clean up after themselves. They leave a lot behind, and we were the little scavengers along with a lot of Filipinos that hiked through the tall cogon grass on the outskirts of Manila looking for pistols, rifles, bayonets, and shell casings. We tried to avoid the live ammunition that was also in abundance. In one field we found the remains of a B-24 Liberator bomber that had crashed; we were able to strip her of many of her instruments, including the compass and flight-level indicators — all intact. In Manila Bay dozens of Japanese ships had been scuttled in a line over a mile long to form a breakwater. Aboard the ships were Jeeps, tanks, large guns, and lots of ammunition. Almost daily scavengers were inadvertently killed in their attempts to remove the ammunition. We were much smarter than that. We sailed our boats out from the Manila Yacht Club to the line of ships and brought our BB guns and a pair of goggles with us so that we could play a game of war with our friends. We would shoot each other as we ran around the decks of the ships and get big welts all over our bodies. We thought we were playing it safe: we were wearing goggles, after all, and not playing with the ammo.

I managed to collect an impressive cache of weapons, which I displayed all over my bedroom walls and on shelves and in closets. We even brought home an antiaircraft gun in our little red wagon. It was in working order but without the base. I had a Springfield and an M-1 rifle; Japanese and American pistols, including a German Luger pistol; lots of bayonets; a Japanese sword; shell casings; practice shells filled with sand; and instruments from the planes. It was an arsenal that would be the envy of every little boy in those days or any other.

All of this ended one Sunday afternoon. We were at the Polo Club, which was just a mile away from a small Philippine Army base. We were swimming in the pool when we heard a small pop. A few minutes later we heard sirens; then the word reached us that two American boys and a Philippine Army guard had been killed while they were playing with a hand grenade at the gate of the Army base. Soon we heard their names; the word spread like wildfire through Manila. Both of them were in Peter's class — and our classes had less than thirty students, so we were a very close-knit group. When we got home, our parents had already been completely informed of the tragedy. My mother ordered our cook, Pedro, to take all of the weapons out of my room and throw them in Manila Bay. The loss of our two friends superseded the loss of the valuable weapons, so there was nothing to really say or do, and I never collected any more artifacts after that.

The Bullfights

For a short period of time the city of Manila decided to build a bullfight ring. This was around 1954 to 1955, and it only lasted a little more than a year. I believe there are only two types of bullfighting: the Portuguese and Spanish methods. The first fights that came to Manila were the Portuguese system, where the bulls were fought on horseback, without padding, and were not killed. This took great horsemanship with horses that could accelerate instantly and stop on a dime, turn and maneuver, and take heavy blows without fear. They wore heavy padding on both sides to protect them from being gored. The picadors would weaken the neck of the bull by sticking the picks into it, the same as the Spanish bullfighters. Picadors were on foot and used capes to taunt the bull and place the picks. The matadors (on horseback) then proceeded to chase the bull around the ring and, with a great flourish, stuck the larger picks into the bull's neck.

Bullfights in Manila, 1954

This was all very beautiful and showed great skill and horsemanship, but there was not enough blood and gore to please the crowds. The horses were sold to the members of the Manila Polo Club who found that these beautiful, responsive animals made perfect polo ponies and with a little training were the pride of the polo club. In the meantime Spanish-style bullfighting was introduced. The bullfighters were not the most famous matadors in Spain; they were more courageous than skilled and mostly came from Mexican bull rings. It usually took them several attempts to put the bull down, which frequently was messy, with the bull enduring a great deal of suffering before it died.

A picador showing off in the ring

Filipinos did not demonstrate great emotion when they saw sporting events, concerts, and other kinds of entertainment such as bullfights. They loved them and filled stadiums and theaters, which often confused the entertainers, who felt they were not appreciated. When Harry Belafonte performed in Manila, he couldn't even get the audience to respond to his famous "Matilda," so he became disappointed and angry — until he read the reviews in the newspaper the next day, which said that they loved him. The same thing happened at the bullfights. Even though there was blood and gore, there was very little reaction from the people, so they decided to add more events to spice it up a little.

Most of the spice came from the idiots of the high school class at the American School. In between fights the organizers held contests where you could do dumb things and possibly get hurt for a small amount of money if you did not run and escape before the end of the trick. They made these spectacles only slightly safer by putting hard leather pads over the horns of the bull. If the bull attempted to gore you, it was more like ramming a baseball bat into your body than a

A matador performing a pass at the arena in Manila

sharp instrument. There were several different types of tricks or events you could choose, including making passes with a large cape, standing on a barrel until the bull knocked it out from under you, or trying to pluck a 100-peso bill from the bull's horn.

Peter was one of the first dummies to try this. He decided to try to make some passes with the cape. There were two kinds of passes we could do: one called the verónica and the other, the gaoneras. In the verónica you put the cape in front of you and to your side and let the bull sweep by in a graceful motion. In the gaoneras you held the cape behind your back with one hand and the other extended outward from your side. This, of course, exposed your body to the bull, and you had to step aside quickly as he passed by. Each successful pass of the verónica would earn you 20 pesos, while the gaoneras earned double that amount. It wasn't until you were in the ring with the bull that you realized how large and powerful an animal he was.

Peter stepped into the ring with the cape and he made two beautiful verónica passes, then tried the much more difficult and dangerous gaoneras. I was actually filming this entire procedure with an 8-millimeter camera when the bull hit Peter square on. He wrapped his arms around both horns and went for the ride of his life. The bull shook him, banged him on the ground, and generally beat him into a pulp. The picadors grabbed the bull by the tail until Peter finally let go and ran away.

Even though Peter beat me up all the time, I was very concerned, and the movie was a disaster: I was shaking that badly. The camera was pointing everywhere except where he was. There are glimpses of him in the movie, but sadly the whole event was not recorded well. His clothes were torn, and he was bleeding, with multiple scratches and bruises all over his body, so we got in a taxi and took him home. My mother was not quite prepared, and after she saw him and heard what he had done, collapsed and almost fainted. After cleaning him up, she and Pop scolded us and forbade us to ever go to the bullfights again.

Spectators competing with the bull

To a teenager, this of course is an invitation to disobey and return.

One of my best friends was Dennis Huth. Dennis's father was the Associated Press correspondent for the Philippines, so he had press access to almost everything, including the bullfights. Dennis was able to obtain several passes, and we were off to the fights again. This time Dennis and I decided to try to stand on the barrels while the picadors shook their capes behind us to draw the bull to charge the barrels. We were standing frozen still to do the opposite, but the bull finally made a charge at my barrel. A split-second before he hit it, I jumped and lost my 20 pesos. Dennis also jumped, so we decided to try something else.

We developed a plan to get the 100-peso bill off the bull's horn. Dennis was a little chunky and not as fast a runner as I was. He was going to take off and run for one of the four barricades around the inside of the ring where you could slide in and be protected. These barricades were close enough to the wall of the arena that the bull could not stick his head and body in. While the bull was chasing Dennis, I was going to run alongside the animal, grab the 100-peso bill from his horn, and make him chase me, at which point Dennis could get behind the barricade while I ran for another barricade.

Our plan had a glitch.

The bull began to chase Dennis, but when I came up alongside, he ignored me. That meant I couldn't get the hundred pesos, and the bull nearly ran over

Dennis, who just barely made it behind the barricade. While the bull was trying to jam his head into the barricade, I came in the other side. Dennis and I looked at the bull whose horns were partially in the opening with the 100-peso bill easily within our reach. We plucked it off, jumped over the arena wall, and made a hasty retreat. Unfortunately, the officials were blocking our way and told us that we had not earned the money correctly, and they took it away from us.

Fortunately the bullfights didn't last long in Manila. They were a festive, colorful, and intriguing event that was however marred with the suffering and death of these magnificent beasts. I still remember them dragging off the dead bulls with a rope tied around their back legs to a Jeep that pulled them through a gate in the arena wall with a trail of blood behind them. It was not a pretty sight.

You Load Sixteen Tons, and What Do You Get?

When we were seniors in high school, Peter and I got a job through my dad during our summer break. We were to work in the Philippine iron mines on the island of Mindoro, one of the larger islands in the Philippine Archipelago.

An open pit mine has narrow roads that wind into an area where earth movers with monster shovels excavate the surface. The shovels load 20 tons of ore into very large trucklike machines that haul it several miles away to crushers, like the song "Sixteen Tons" by Merle Travis. The machines had tires with a 10-foot diameter, and the operator sat in a cab above that. The trick is to get these huge machines turned around on the narrow road.

The solution was the LeTourneau Tournahauler. My dad sold a number of them to the mine, which is how we got the jobs to drive the machines. The unique features of the hauler were that each wheel had its own electric motor powered by a large generator in the front unit. The generator and cab were separated from the ore bucket with a swivel mechanism that would allow the front and back to operate independently. It was possible to lock the front wheels and drive the back wheels forward to fold up the machine. To turn around on the narrow road, we folded the unit up, turned it around, and then spread it back out so it was facing the road in the direction it came from. The shovel would fill the bucket and then the hauler was on its way.

Two special features of the Tournahauler were the steering system and the speed control. Speed was controlled by either a hand lever or a foot pedal. There was no steering wheel. To steer, there was a toggle switch on the dashboard which would turn the front end left or right. You held on to a bar and used your thumbs to steer. The steering wasn't smooth: it sort of jerked from one direction to another. To soften the ride, the operator would sit on about ten inches of foam.

We practiced for a few days with a professional and then came the big day to solo. I executed everything well and turned around, got my load of ore, and wound my way up the quarry to the main dirt road.

That's when things got out of control. These big babies would hit a top speed of around 30 mph, and the road was pretty straight, so I put the pedal to the metal. Soon I began to bounce on all that foam and soft rubber tires, and when I came down my foot would hit the gas pedal. The whole system began to resonate, and I started to fly up and down holding onto the bar and trying to operate the steering toggle, the front end swerving wildly from one direction to the other.

There was another problem. The trip to the crusher passed through a small barrio or village. The barrio was just ahead and they saw this monster machine heading toward them out of control. People were screaming, and the pigs and chickens were running around and it was total mayhem. I got control just before wiping out the village by remembering to use the hand throttle to stop the resonating. I went straight to the crusher, dumped my load and tried to sort of hide for a while. It is not an easy thing to hide a 10-ton machine, and I was soon summoned to explain to the managers what happened. They made me go with an instructor for another two days before going solo again.

FLORETTA: CRUISING THE PHILIPPINE ARCHIPELAGO

Peter and I were good friends with Peter and Patrick Parsons, two of the four sons of Chick and Katsy. Commander Chick Parsons was a U.S. naval commander who was one of the primary officers in charge of organizing the resistance against the Japanese in the Philippines. At one time he was actually shot out of a submarine torpedo tube in order to make a secret landing on one of the Philippine islands. His efforts during the war earned him the love and respect of the Filipino people, and he was made an honorary citizen of the country. He also loved the Filipino people and decided the Philippines would be his permanent home. He moved his family to Manila where he built a home and a business that was very successful. His business, named the Luzon Stevedoring Company, had a fleet of tugboats and later expanded into other lines of business such as the distillation of alcohol. With the success of the business, Chick converted a 110-foot naval patrol boat into a yacht he named *Floretta*.

Sisiman Cove: Shark!

We lived only a block away from the Parsons and spent a lot of time together. We frequently went along on the *Floretta* to some of the wonderful beaches and reefs around the southern part of Luzon. A favorite beach on the Bataan Peninsula was Sisiman Cove, which had only a narrow entrance to a deep, clear pool surrounded by a high cliff. We would climb up the rock wall of the cliff and dive into the pool below. One time a four-foot sand shark swam into the pool while we watched. Of course, there was an immediate challenge between us to see who would dare to dive into the pool. The two Peters, being older than Patrick and I, took up the challenge and climbed up the wall where they grabbed their knees and jumped in to make a pair of cannon balls. They were almost running on the water to get out — and the shark was just about as fast getting out of the pool to open water where there were no nutty kids disturbing his explorations.

Shark Tales: Hammerhead and a Manta Ray

Another shark tale happened while cruising on the *Floretta*; this one, a little more frightening. Patrick was driving the motorboat tender we carried and pulling Peter Parsons on skis around the *Floretta*. Suddenly a huge manta ray with a 20-foot wingspan emerged out of the water, way out in front of the motorboat. His wings came out of the water with a huge splash, followed by a giant hammerhead shark leaping out of the water in pursuit of the ray. Patrick was looking backward watching Peter on the skis, so he didn't see what was happening in front of the boat. Peter, however, had a good view and knew that this was not a time to fall off. Aboard the *Floretta* we could see it all, with the motorboat heading right for the big chase. We blew the ship's whistle, but Patrick never veered course and went right over the two water beasts, followed by Peter. The wings of the ray could have overturned the boat and certainly the skier, but all ended fine and possibly helped the escape of the ray from the horror of the hammerhead.

Shark Tales: Part Three

At the entrance to Manila Bay, there were some very nice areas for swimming and diving. I was with Patrick Parsons and my brother. We had taken the dinghy from the *Floretta* out with one of the girls to go diving and take some pictures. We mostly used to go free diving and would take pictures with a waterproof camera. Suddenly a big shark swam by, sending all of us scrambling back into the dinghy. In the frenzy, we dropped the camera. We did paper, rock, scissors and the girl lost. It was not one of our most chivalrous moments, but we three guys happily stayed in the boat while we sent her to go get the camera with the shark looming around.

Buzzed by Bats; Chased Away by Poisonous Sea Snakes

The *Floretta* became our home for almost two months when we went on an extended trip through the Philippine Archipelago and on to Borneo and Bali in Indonesia. The year was 1955, and the two Peters had just finished high school and would be going off to college.

This was an experience none of us will ever forget. The journey took us to some of the strangest places, and we saw and did what few people will ever get the chance to do.

On Palawan there is an underwater river that is over two miles long and can be entered by a small boat from the sea. As we got deep into the cave, we were buzzed by thousands of bats, shrieking and screaming at us intruders. It was pretty frightening, and the girls on board were in a panic except cool Katsy. That evening when we were back on board, hundreds of sea snakes swam around the boat and tried to slither up the sides but could not hold on. Jo Jo Parsons, the youngest of the brothers, still had an ama to take care of him, and she fainted away at the sight of the snakes. They were poisonous, so it was not a time to fool around. We hoisted anchor and got out of there.

Mindanao: Moros, Dopey, and Monkey Hunting

On the biggest island, Mindanao, there were pirates, and the Philippine navy sent a patrol boat to escort us in this Muslim region of the Philippines. The threat to yachts came from fanatical Islamic Moros. They drove large bancas, a single outrigger canoe powered by a 25-horsepower Evinrude with a bazooka in the bow. They would approach a yacht shooting at the waterline to sink the boat, then attack it with guns and knives, killing everyone aboard. The knives had long wavy blades and were called keris. When the Americans had taken over the Philippines from Spain, they found the Moros to be a huge threat and had numerous skirmishes that ended in disasters. The Moros would bind up their whole bodies with cloth strips like a mummy, and wielding their keris would run at the troops and lop their heads off even though they had been shot multiple times. The wrappings cut off their circulation, and they could run another hundred yards after being shot. This was the "mother of necessity" that caused the invention of the .45-caliber pistol. The bullet was so big it would knock the Moros down to stop their deadly attacks. We carried a lot of guns, but it was nice to have the navy with us.

We did go to the biggest city in Mindanao, Zamboanga, where we visited the local market. Among other things, we bought parrots and monkeys. The *Floretta*'s bridge was alive with two large white macaws, my green parrot named Dopey, and a monkey with a tail, contradicting the words of the song, "The Monkeys Have No Tails in Zamboanga" by Harry McClintock. Dopey was a wonderful bird and stayed with me until I went to college in the United States. He slept on the edge of my bed, ate dinner with us sitting on the back of my chair, and always sat on my shoulder when I was at home.

The rainforests in Mindanao were filled with huge trees, logged for their hardwoods. When we were there, the logging had still left most of the monster trees; these were loaded with monkeys that were supposedly quite mean and good to eat. A hunting party— consisting of six of us boys and some of the crew, armed with M-16s, a Thompson submachine gun, and some pistols— went into the jungle to hunt wild boar and monkeys. We knew nothing about hunting and very little about guns. After taking pot shots at the monkeys, we heard the grunt of a wild boar charging through the brush. Patrick had the machine gun and let loose at the noise. The Thompson kicked up in the air, and Patrick started to spray the trees with their long vines. We were all diving for cover when one of the vines was severed and came crashing down almost killing us. Pure mayhem. One of my pot shots hit a monkey, and he fell down dead. He did not look mean to me. I felt terrible and never hunted again.

Turtle Islands, Warring Monkey Kingdom, Borneo, Bali

The Turtle Islands gave us a treat since we arrived just when the giant turtles had laid their eggs on the beach and buried them under the sand. We could see them all heading toward the sea after burying the eggs. When the eggs hatched, the baby turtles would dash to the sea and hope gulls and other predators would not get them before they entered the water. The eggs were about the size of a chicken egg, but perfectly round, and looked like a ping-pong ball. They had soft shells, and being bad boys we played ball with some of them and bounced them off walls to see how much it would take to break them. They were very tough but not tougher than a 14-year-old troublemaker. Fortunately the Turtle Islands are not on the beaten path, and few people ever went there.

Another remote island was home for two kingdoms of monkeys on opposite sides of the island. There was no question as to who was one of the kings. He was old and grizzly and very large and strong. He sat on top of a rock, and every once in a while a younger male would make an attempt to dethrone him. It usually took one big swat, and the challenger was history. The king also enjoyed a harem, his females surrounding him and giving him great attention, picking lice and grooming him. We could actually walk among them, since they had no fear of humans at the time. According to our guide, sometimes the two sides warred against each other.

In Borneo we stopped at Sandakan and later Balikpapan. We rented bikes in Sandakan and soon discovered that they drove on the left-hand side of the road as we faced a horde of speeding cars. Navigating the roundabouts was also a trick, but we managed to stay alive. There was an insurrection going on in Balikpapan. After we got shot at a few times, we decided to leave in a hurry. There was a big Shell Oil refinery there, and it appeared that the insurgents were trying to damage it.

Bali was a treat. It was a beautiful island, and the best part for young men were the women, who generally were topless. As we drove around, we would whistle a little tune when we saw a nice one so that Katsy wouldn't know what it was all about. Mothers know everything, and we were not fooling her, but she let us have our fun. A famous painter lived there, and we visited with him, and Katsy bought one of his paintings. There were temples and great masks with long tongues and huge eyeballs to scare the demons. There was a shallow cave where a dog lived along with hundreds of bats. The bats filled the cave with dung, which the dog seemed to live on. Yuck!

The adventures and sights never seemed to end on the *Floretta*. It was the trip of a lifetime and brought the world of fantasy to reality. These things really do exist, and the complexity of the world and its creatures made my faith in God become more clear.

Chick Parsons and Peter Harken relaxing on the Floretta

Pop on the Floretta

Peter and Olaf hunting in Mindanao

Sailing in Manila Bay

Our time spent on the Parsons' boat, Floretta

Chapter Three

Georgia Tech, UW-Madison, and Alpine Skiing: Why Wisconsin? (1957–1963)

COLLEGE YEARS

In the fall of 1957 I sat in the LeTourneau Amphitheater outside of Atlanta where the incoming freshman class was getting an orientation on how to be college students at Georgia Tech. The most memorable part was when the speaker said, "Look to your left and then to your right. One of you three will not be here at the end of the next quarter." You would think that with a warning like that, you'd hit the books really hard.

Not me.

Pop had given me enough money to pay for my tuition and basic needs for two quarters. Somehow I managed to spend all of the money the first quarter, most of it on partying and gadgets like amplifiers and speakers. I had pledged Lambda Chi Alpha fraternity, and most of the brothers there were pretty good at partying. But being older and wiser, they also knew they had to study. Tech was one of the top-rated engineering schools in the nation, and the faculty were not going to let you graduate without really knowing your subject.

When I got my midterm grades — Fs and Ds and Cs — I could see that I was in real trouble. I wasn't sure how to get out of this, so I called my American School friend Charlie Clark, who was attending Emory University in Atlanta. I knew from high school he was a real brain and studying to be a doctor. Charlie said, "I want you to come to my uncle's farm over Thanksgiving, and you're going to do a marathon of studying with my help."

It worked, and I survived the first quarter. I learned a good lesson, which kept me out of trouble for the next four years, letting me graduate with a bachelor of science degree in Industrial Engineering.

Bogenville *Freighter: A Tough Job*

My Dad put me through college, but I had to work to keep my head above water for other expenses. Going home to Manila during summer vacation was one of them. My friend Donnie helped me line up a job on a Norwegian freighter that would travel from San Francisco to Manila.

I had very little money left, so I needed the job and I had to get myself from Georgia to San Francisco. I took a bus for part of the trip, and hitchhiked the rest of the way. 2600 miles later, I found my way to the Lambda Chi Alpha fraternity house on the Berkeley campus. I was able to stay for free for the two nights before the ship left. The guys from the house gave me a ride to the port where the ship, *Bogenville*, was docked. By the time I got to the ship, I had 50 cents left to my name.

The shipping unions are very strong and problematic at times. I watched as a drunk crane operator was trying to load a printing press onto the ship. They couldn't get him off the crane, he refused. They couldn't fire him or make him go home to sleep it off. He ended up dropping the whole printing press straight into the drink. They had to stop all the operations to try to get the drunk off his seat. It was disgusting to see how the shipping union operated and nothing could be done.

The bosun mate didn't like me when I got there and put me on the team with the guys that did one of the dirtiest, hardest jobs on the ship. The big sheaves used for craning freight up and down had to be cleaned and lubed. They would drop them down to us, where we would have to pull the bearing apart, put a big gob of grease in it, grease the cable, put it back together, and lift it back up to hook on the big shackle. We also had to chip paint around the hatches, along with a number of other maintenance tasks.

They were tough jobs, but it got me home to Manila with some money in my pocket. The ship went on through the archipelago, turned around, and was back in Manila in about a month. So I had that long to go see my family before I got back on for the return trip from Manila to San Francisco. Donnie was on board for that trip and would come down to flirt with us while the guys were working. One of the guys was in the middle of hoisting a sheave back up, saw her and dropped the rope. We caught the line just before the sheave hit the deck, but after that the bosun mate suggested she not come down where the guys were working.

That trip back was tough. We were carrying copra, which is a combustive, but valuable coconut derivative. One of my jobs was chipping paint — special care had to be taken not to make any sparks with our tools, which made us pretty nervous. We managed to make it back without blowing anything up and I got myself back to Georgia in time for the fall semester.

Lambda Chi Alpha and the Beer Runs

I'm not really as close to my college fraternity brothers and friends as to my high school classmates in Manila. I think the main reason for this was that I lost my two best friends from college shortly after I got out of the Navy and moved to Wisconsin. Dick Warner, an architectural student, roomed with me for a couple of years, and we did a lot of things together. He later became a pilot for United Airlines and then passed away from cancer a few years later. Jimmy Urquhart, a textile-engineering student, was my other close friend and had a prankish sense of humor that kept folks on their toes. I lost touch with Jimmy after he moved to Tennessee.

We had some adventures. One time, we drove to Florida to pick up as much beer as we could carry in Dick's little blue Mini Cooper. Georgia had blue laws, and you couldn't buy a beer after nine o'clock. We had planned to open a business in the fraternity house after nine o'clock where we would sell beer at a real premium to our thirsty compadres. We had two extra passengers, Harold Brown, one of our fraternity brothers, and Nebbish, my little dog. With the trunk and the insides full of cases of beer, we crossed the Georgia line and headed for Atlanta. Harold, who was driving, fell asleep on the expressway. The car veered to the left and went down into the embankment, where it rolled over. The first words spoken were,

"Is Nebbish all right?"

She was, and so was everyone else.

We did have a problem, though. We were transporting booze over the state line that did not have Georgia tax stamps on the cans. If the police came, we'd be in real trouble. The four of us, together with a number of other people who'd stopped to help, rolled the car upright and managed to push it up the embankment onto the road. In order to do this, we had to unload all the beer. You never saw a group work so fast or so hard. Soon we were going down the road with a broken front windshield and a squashed roof. Harold lived between Atlanta and where we were, so we stopped at his house and hid the car in his garage and took his parents' car back to school.

We were back in business for the weekend parties.

Frequently we consumed quite a bit of our own stock. On one football-Saturday morning, Dick was so hungover he couldn't wake up. We took his bed and put it in the middle of the street in front of the fraternity house. We then carefully carried him out and laid him on the bed. With all of the football traffic, he soon caused a traffic jam, and cars started to honk at him. This, of course, woke him up, and he was so bewildered, it took him a minute or two to orient himself and run for the house.

Nebbish and the Cherry Bomb

My little dog, Nebbish, went everywhere with me. A girl I knew had given her to me, and this dog was so cute and smart that I had to keep her. She was a cross between a dachshund and a cocker spaniel. In other words, she had long hair and a long body. She lived in the dorm with me, and used to follow me to class then patiently wait outside until I finished.

In our senior year, we moved into the attic of the fraternity house. Nebbish came with. It was a spacious area, and we decorated it with a fine assortment of Playboy Playmate of the Month posters. Having a dog was against the rules, but almost everybody loved Nebbish and tolerated her.

One day Nebbish was a little too hungry and jumped up on one of the dining-room tables after they had been set but before the brothers had come in to eat. She was busy downing some Southern catfish when she was spotted.

There are always a couple of jerks who hate everything and use the rules to reinforce their position instead of using compassion and common sense. They caused enough of a stir that Nebbish was banned from the fraternity house at the next meeting.

I did not attend, since I was on the roof with a cherry bomb. I had determined beforehand that the chief bozo would be sitting with his back to the chimney. I dropped the cherry bomb down the chimney, and it blew a hole in his pants and blackened his backsides. When he recovered, he was fighting mad and ran up to my room where I was busy studying at my desk. I couldn't contain myself when he turned around and showed the damage, and I laughed until my sides hurt. He swore up and down, but he couldn't prove anything. A few weeks later I found a great home on a farm for Nebbish and heard that she was very happy with her new family.

Educating Roger

The fraternity had a staff run by the housemother, a chief cook, and a "houseboy" who cleaned all the shared areas. Roger was our houseboy. He was a big young strapping black man with a great personality and a sharp wit. After his normal routine, he would frequently come into the attic and play cards with us.

We soon recognized that he was pretty intelligent and started to ask him about his education and background. He was a high-school graduate but told us that he got through school by playing football, where he was a star player. We then asked him some simple math, English, history, and geography questions. We were shocked at how little he knew and how he possibly could have graduated from high school. He did not know the difference between the brown and the blue on a map and had very little understanding of where Atlanta was in the world. He was barely able to add simple numbers, and it was apparent that our educational system was sorely lacking.

We wanted to provide him an education better suited to his intelligence, so each of us took a subject to teach him. I took geography. We spent almost three months working with Roger five or more days a week in the evening. He was like a sponge. He soaked up the information as fast as we could feed it to him. He was very smart, and it would have been devastating to see such a good mind go to waste. At the end of three months he could name all the capitals of the United States and most of the countries of the world and their capitals. He was doing basic trigonometry, reading *To Kill a Mockingbird* and other books, and had a pretty good understanding of the history of the United States. He knew who our leaders were, including the state senators and governor of Georgia.

Roger was fired, partially because he had contracted gonorrhea but mostly because the Southern boys didn't like an educated black man (Equal Employment Opportunity didn't exist yet). I was delighted to see him one day driving a three-wheel motorbike with the name of a pharmacy on it. He'd met the pharmacist getting his medicine for gonorrhea and impressed him so much that he hired him and started him on the path to a college education and pharmacy school.

Summer Job: "Working on the Railroad"

I learned the definition of hard work between work on the freighter and the railroad. During my third year in college, I worked for a few months at Southern Railroad. The father of my friend Bonnie was the head of rail welding, and helped me get the job. The hours were from 8 p.m. to 8 a.m.; the work was grinding the welds of a continuous rail system. They would roll the rails in on a train car and lay them down as it went along. The welders would weld them together, and we would follow in two-man teams to grind the joints smooth.

The old guys didn't like us young bucks coming into their territory and wanted to be unionized to protect their jobs from the younger generation. So to try and drive us out, they would aim their grinders forward to make the sparks shoot up under our plastic visors. We could have retaliated, but knew it wasn't a fight we were going to win since they had a lot more experience and better aim. Eventually they learned to accept us, or maybe it was because they knew we were only there for the summer and weren't going to take their jobs away from them.

Georgia Tech in the Civil Rights Era

I went to Georgia Tech at a historic time. The University of Alabama was ordered to integrate, which caused riots and mayhem. The National Guard was called out, and Alabama's governor, George Wallace, defied the president of the United States and the U.S. attorney general. All of this racism was new to me: we'd been raised in a mixed society, which seemed perfectly natural to us.

Shortly after Alabama, the University of Georgia was ordered to integrate. It had some similar problems but not quite to the same extent as the University of Alabama. The Ku Klux Klan was out in force, trying to scare black men from entering the school. They managed to accomplish the integration, though there was some rioting. Tech was next. The chancellor of the university called a meeting of the entire student body, faculty, and staff members in a building called the Dome, where basketball games were held. Everyone was checked for identification, and no one was allowed in aside from the students or faculty working for the university. A sea of reporters grew outside, along with the Ku Klux Klan and the curious. The doors were locked, and the chancellor made a short speech. He told us that three Negro students were going to enter the college the following day. He then said that any student or faculty or employee who spoke to a reporter or anyone else outside of the building, or who disrupted or impaired the movement of the three students, would be automatically expelled or fired. The following day the Ku Klux Klan surrounded the entire campus but had to keep their hoods up according to a new law. They tried to taunt the students into talking. But there was not a whisper, and integration happened totally without incident.

While I was there, women were also allowed to enter the university. The only incident that happened was a panty raid on the second night of their enrollment that seemed to have been fun for everyone.

Parting Ways

Karen and Dick, Bonnie and Jimmy, and I, with whomever I was dating at the time, hung out together everywhere and were inseparable friends. We played Kingston Trio records and sang along until we knew every song. We partied together, studied together, taught Roger together, shared feelings, and they constantly tried to fix me up with girls. They did a pretty good job of that; it was like having a private dating service. After graduation we all did our own things, but stayed in contact. Dick married Karen; Jimmy married Bonnie; and I went into the Navy and got married, too.

Dick, who was often referred to as "Honey" for some strange reason, was a United Airlines pilot based out of Chicago. He and Karen had four children when Dick became ill with cancer shortly after becoming a second officer. When he was no longer qualified to fly with his cancer, he managed a golf course until he passed away. Karen has had a difficult life but managed with the help of her kids.

Jimmy and Bonnie also had four children. Jimmy took off with another woman, and we lost contact ever since. It was hard for me to believe that he would do that. Bonnie and I remained close friends until she recently passed away. I helped her buy a bed and breakfast called the Aberdeen Inn in Ashville, North Carolina. It's a beautiful house with five bedrooms and two additional rooms in an attached cottage with a big wraparound porch and beautiful antique furniture. Bonnie gave it the warmth, humor, and hospitality that made it special. It had been difficult, but she made it work, and we sold it some years ago for a good profit.

Losing these friends made me lose my connection with Georgia Tech and Lambda Chi. I've only been to the new house once in all of these years. The campus is very different and much bigger; the house has completely been rebuilt; and Atlanta is so different that I can't find my way around. There was one big skyscraper in 1960. Now there are dozens.

Tacking Towards Wisconsin

By the time I graduated from Georgia Tech in 1963, I'd fulfilled my five-year residency obligation to become a naturalized American citizen. I attended the ceremony in Atlanta, where I gave up my Dutch citizenship to become an American — a proud moment for me.

From there I went to Madison, Wisconsin, where I waited patiently to get accepted into the U.S. Navy Officer Candidate School so that I could become a Navy officer. Because of my very international background, the security check took a long time. Unfortunately and fortunately I'd gone skiing with some friends and had broken my leg. While I was waiting to get into OCS, the U.S. Army drafted me. When I showed up with my leg and arm in a cast, the Army drafting officer could hardly believe it and sent me home to heal. Two weeks later I was accepted into OCS.

Today, when I think about it, breaking my leg might have saved my life; otherwise, I would have been a foot soldier on the ground in Vietnam instead of a Navy officer on a ship off the Vietnamese coast.

So how did I break my leg? And why Wisconsin?

Once again, I'm getting ahead of my story. Let's go back to 1955, the year Peter left the Philippines for college in the United States.

A Very Good Idea

In Manila, we had a family friend named Bob Dudley who lived nearby. He was one of the Flying Dudleys of Wausau, four brothers who became famous Navy pilots during World War II. Three of them, including Bob, entered the Navy through the Flying Badgers program at the University of Wisconsin at Madison.

When Peter started looking at colleges, Bob contacted the UW swimming coach on Peter's behalf. "I think you ought to take a look at this guy," Bob told the coach. Peter had other prospects, too, including Stanford. But he and Pop included Wisconsin in their tour of schools.

Peter remembers that tour: "When I got to the campus at Madison and looked at that lake and the sailing and all the bars and stuff downtown, being a very undisciplined kid, I told my dad, 'I think I should go here.'" Pop wasn't so sure. He knew damn well what motivated Peter, but he also recognized that with the swimming scholarship, it was the best deal.

"I don't think you're going to make it here," Pop told him. "But if you do make it at this school with all these distractions, you'll be able to make it anywhere in life."

Sure enough, Peter's scholarship lasted only two years. He became active in Madison's Hoofers Club, whose members did all sorts of outdoor activities: mountain climbing, whitewater canoeing, horsemanship, and sailing. Winter sports enthralled Peter the most. Coming from the tropics, we'd never done any of those. People thought he was crazy, but Mom being a Swede and Pop being Dutch, the DNA was in us. So it was then that Peter discovered iceboating and skiing.

By his sophomore year, Peter's coach could see that he was doing things besides swimming — activities that caused him to stiffen up in the pool. One day the coach called him aside. "I want to know what else you're doing," he said. Peter told him.

"Well, you can't do that," the coach said. "I'm going to give you two weeks. You make up your mind." For a little while longer, Peter tried to rededicate himself to swimming — while still sneaking off to do the other stuff. Finally, he fessed up. "Coach," he said, "it's not in me anymore. My heart's gone."

And so, quite suddenly, was his scholarship to the University of Wisconsin.

Pop had given both Peter and me the same deal: He'd support us as long as we were in school and our grades were decent. Well, now Peter was calling our dad, back home in Manila, with a different idea. He had it all worked out. Sure, he'd just quit the swim team and lost his scholarship. But now he had something better in mind: he would go out to Aspen and learn how to ski really well.

"Some day I might be in the North Woods somewhere, God knows where, be trapped in the ice and the snow and everything, and have to learn how to get out of it and save myself," he told our dad. "So it would be good for me to go to Colorado, because we never learned this kind of stuff in the Philippines."

Pop was pretty good at listening to us. He would just stay very quiet. I mean, here's this smart-assed kid trying to buffalo a guy who's spent four and a half years in one of the most horrible prison camps in the world and survived.

"Son," said Pop after a long pause, "I think that's a very good idea. Good luck. Let me know when you're back."

Click.

"Daaaad. . . ."

Peter was talking into a dead phone line. That was it. He had about 50 bucks to his name, and all his parental support had just been cut off. So what did he do? Gathered up a whole pile of peanut-butter-and-jelly sandwiches and his dog, and loaded them into his crappy old '51 Chevy convertible — with the top down to fit his crummy skis — and headed west.

"By the time I landed in Aspen," he said, "I had six inches of snow in the car, and my dog and I were huddled up in the sleeping bag."

How Peter made his way, with entry-level newspaper and motel-maintenance work until he hooked up with the U.S. Olympic Team and truly learned to ski (according to the Black-and-Blue Method), is a story for another time. What's important for the present narrative — still twenty years before that fateful meeting in the Avalon Hotel bar in Miami Beach — is that Peter did eventually return to Madison, this time on shaky ground with the university faculty, no support from our father, and no money whatsoever. The kid needed a job.

The job he found was with Gilson Medical Electronics, whose owner was active in the Hoofers Club. Though Peter ultimately graduated with a degree in international economics, he'd taken some engineering courses at the university. Dr. Gilson hired him as an engineer and draftsman.

With the iceboating and the sailing and the position in Gilson's shop, plus a healthy dose of reality, all the pieces were coming into place for the beginning of an upstart outfit that would become the world's largest sailboat-hardware manufacturer.

Looking Like a Civil War Veteran

All of which begins to explain what I was doing in Wisconsin and how I broke my leg. After college, I moved into the Lambda Chi house near the university in Madison and did some work with Peter at Gilson, while I waited for news from the Navy.

As for that leg...

There were six of us in my big blue DeSoto with the tail fins (about which I'll have more to tell). Three girls and three guys — we were going up to Indianhead Mountain to ski. As we left, I told them, "Let's not forget to put oil in the car at the first gas stop." We were having a great time talking and laughing and sleeping, and of course we forgot to put oil in when we stopped for gas. We drove all night and reached our cabin early the next morning. We put on our ski clothes, and off we went to the hill, about 10 miles from our cabin. We had a great time skiing, and in the late afternoon drove back to the cabin, but we didn't quite make it. The engine froze up solid, completely dry of oil. There was nothing to do but leave the car there, get some more skiing in, then find different people to take us back to Madison.

Searching the junkyards in Madison, I finally found an engine that would fit the big DeSoto. I borrowed my friend Bob Ream's red pickup truck, took a couple of girls with me and our skis and we headed back to Indianhead. I delivered the engine to the local Chrysler dealer in Ironwood, Michigan.

We then headed for the ski hill. It was now early spring, and the weather had warmed up quite a bit. There were clumps of grass coming out of the snow, and I was skiing on black diamond runs that were far above my capabilities — I didn't know how to ski except for the lesson Peter gave me. Schussing down the hill and out of control, my ski dug into a clump of grass, and I went flying head over heels when I heard a big crack. My tibia was broken. The ski patrol brought me to a local hospital; after surveying the scene, I decided to leave my ski boot on and get the leg fixed at the University of Wisconsin hospital in Madison.

The girls and I loaded our gear into the truck, and I went into the back of the truck since I had to keep my legs stretched out. Fortunately it was warm enough for me to be able to sit back there. But the warm weather also created another problem: the snow was melting rapidly. On one stretch, the entire area had become flooded, and you could barely find the road. I told Barbara Koester, the driver, to be careful not to gun the engine, since the fan would pick up water and short out the distributor. Of course, she panicked and gunned the engine, which killed it and left us stranded in what looked like a lake in the middle of Wisconsin.

I got out of the back of the truck and hobbled around, taking the distributor apart and drying it off. We tried to start the truck to no avail. Finally a large snowplow came by and gave us a tow. The engine started, and we were able to get back to Madison, where I was taken directly to the hospital. They set my leg in a large cast, so I was unable to drive.

Every day Peter drove me to Gilson Medical Electronics where I was also working as a draftsman. I was living in the Lambda Chi Alpha fraternity house at the time. One Saturday night, even though I had not been drinking, I was working my way up the back steps on my crutches when I reached for the door handle at the top of the stairs and started to teeter backward. I catapulted down the stairs and went through a glass window at the bottom of the stairs, leading with my right hand. The glass almost cut my right thumb off, and I was back in the hospital again for a long and very difficult operation.

I could hear the surgeons discussing what to do. They were speaking to someone at Johns Hopkins Hospital in Baltimore who specialized in attaching severed muscles and tendons. They wanted to keep me awake so that they could test out their different connections, and the nurse asked if I would like to see what was going on. Before I could answer, she had me look into the mirror. One quick look at my hand, and I immediately passed out.

They brought me around with smelling salts, and after five hours the thumb was reattached and put into a large cast to keep it from moving. I now had my right leg in a cast and my right hand in a cast. This was not good; I couldn't get around on my crutches. I couldn't do anything. Peter made me a special crutch that fit on my elbow, which helped. I was not a very happy person at that time.

Finally after several weeks the mechanic up in Ironwood notified me that the engine was back in my car: I could come up and get it. So I took the train as far north as it would go, looking like a Civil War veteran. I then hitchhiked on a milk truck to retrieve my car.

Fortunately the DeSoto had push-button shifting on the left side of the steering wheel — one of the very few cars that did. I used my left hand for steering and shifting, and my left foot for accelerator and brakes. My right leg was stretched out on the seat, and I managed to get the car back to Madison with no further problems. As I said before, the good news was that during this time I was drafted and had a great excuse to not have to go. The other good fortune was that the cast came off my hand and my leg just before I had to leave for OCS.

Chapter Four

The Navy Years: With Some Tinkering on the Side (1963–1966)

AN OFFICER. BUT A GENTLEMAN?

It was a day I will never forget: November 22, 1963. I had just graduated from the U.S. Navy Officer Candidate School in Newport, Rhode Island. It was an emotional day, since we'd gone through a lot of very intense training, and today we were going to become officers and gentlemen in the United States Navy.

Ensign Olaf Harken, 1963

As I drove off in my big DeSoto on my way back to Wisconsin, I heard the awful news that President Kennedy, my new commander in chief, had been shot in Dallas. People on the highway were signaling each other to turn on their radios. Everyone was in great shock. Having just graduated, this was enormously upsetting to me. I had to pull off to the side of the road to listen to the

USS Forster *DER 334*

broadcast. I drove through the night with the radio on, listening to the news: the confirmation that the president had died, the inauguration of President Johnson, all the terrible details. When I got to Wisconsin, I met with my brother and friends, who along with the rest of the nation were glued to their radios and televisions listening in disbelief to what was happening.

After that initial shock, followed by two weeks of scheduled R&R, I left Madison in the big DeSoto on my way to San Diego for an intense six-week communications training course. Being young and foolish, I thought I could make the trip nonstop but decided to take on a hitchhiker when I started to hallucinate in Arizona.

While we were driving, I learned that the hitchhiker I picked up was on a mission. He had a girlfriend in Phoenix who had cheated on him, and he was going to shoot her lover. He showed me his gun and also mentioned he hated naval officers, since he was a seaman. I was dressed in civilian clothing, but my officer's cap was in the back window. I prayed that he would not look back there, which he did not.

When we got to Phoenix, fortunately I was able to drop him off without any incident and immediately called the police and told them what the situation was without giving them my identity, since I was in a rush to get to San Diego. This little incident woke me up completely for the rest of the trip.

Communication school was pretty easy, and San Diego was a real gas. I made friends easily at the bachelor quarters and a group of us toured the nightspots between San Diego and Tijuana, Mexico, almost every evening. However, the fun had to end sometime, and I was soon on a plane to Pearl Harbor to meet my ship and start my new career as a communications officer aboard the USS *Forster*. When I walked down the pier, I first saw a rather battered old ship with a lot of dents on the side. But she looked like she had fresh paint on her. She was not a very large ship, but she was big in my eyes.

I requested permission to come on board and met the officers who were on duty. Engineering Officer Jim Manion reminded me of Hawkeye in "M.A.S.H." because he immediately tried to convince me to tell the captain that I liked to play bridge. Fortunately Operations Officer Jim Keach told me that the captain was a bridge fanatic and that Manion was trying to get out of having to play with him every night until he had to go on watch, losing Jim hours of needed sleep. When I met Captain Barry, one of the first questions he asked me was if I played bridge. I told him I didn't know anything about it, and I was very sorry but that I'd never played before.

Aboard the Forster

The USS *Forster* DER 334 is named in honor of Edward William Forster, a machinist in the U.S. Navy who was killed in action during the Battle of the Solomon Islands in August 1942. Machinist Forster was wounded while serving aboard the cruiser USS *Vincennes*. He died two days later and was buried at sea from the Australian cruiser *Canberra*.

DER stands for "destroyer escort radar picket ship." She's a small destroyer of approximately 1,250 tons, measuring 306 feet in length and 36 feet at the beam, and carrying a crew of 186 men. The DE is a fairly common ship. The "R" meant that we had an excessive amount of radar, which was used in our job of supplementing the planes, ships, and ground stations forming the Distant Early Warning line that was established between Midway Island and Northern Alaska. This line was constantly patrolled by aircraft and ships, looking for Russian bombers coming from Siberia over the Kamchatka Peninsula and Bering Sea to attack our continent. Our squadron of five ships took turns on station in the North Pacific, with three ships on station at all times. These ships operated in 500-mile circles between Midway Island and Adak, Alaska. Flying above us was a constant stream of radar-carrying Constellation aircraft, nicknamed "Willie Victors," with huge radar domes.

One of our functions was to provide a landing strip in the middle of the North Pacific Ocean in case one of these planes had to come down. The landing strip consisted of a string of lights with a soaplike substance dumped on the sea to calm the waves in the remote chance that they could make a safe landing in seas that normally exceeded six feet and often were in the 20- to 30-foot range. It was more of a psychological boost than a realistic one.

CARS, GIRLS, AND CAPERS

My First Wife

After graduating from OCS, I had two weeks of leave before reporting for duty. Peter was running a Hoofers ski trip to Indianhead Mountain with three busloads of students. One of the great things about the ski trips was the abundance of girls going for some good skiing and romance. I spotted Connie in the back of our bus and soon made my move. It was not smooth, but it eventually worked out. Not too subtly I let her know that I was a dashing naval officer, which didn't seem to impress her. Still, persistence paid off, and we both fell in love.

For the next two years we had a mail romance. After graduating from the University of Wisconsin, she got a job in New York as a floor manager at Macy's. That was no small accomplishment, since Macy's was probably one of the largest department stores in the world. Connie loved New York. She also met plenty of men and, being a very beautiful girl, was romanced. At one point, she fell for one of her suitors. I received a veiled Dear John letter — a huge blow to me. I pleaded for her to wait a short while: I would be coming to San Diego for training for my new job as chief engineer and could fly to New York and see her. She waited. I traveled to New York. We got married at the Unitarian Church in New York, had a reception at the Waldorf Astoria, and left for Hawaii via San Francisco.

Mission accomplished...

Almost.

I had one other matter to deal with. I, too, had gone astray after finding out my true love was teetering in her devotion to me. I had met Leslie Brown, a wonderful girl whose father was a colonel and the commanding officer of Wheeler Army Air Field on the Western side of Oahu. Leslie was funny and warm, and we had a lot of fun together. When I left for San Diego, I gave Leslie the DeSoto to use and take care of while I was gone.

I arrived in Honolulu a few hours before Connie was to arrive since I was on a military flight and she was on a commercial flight. I had arranged for Leslie to pick me up. I told her I needed to talk to her and told her about my marriage. This was extremely painful and made me feel like the cad that I was. I took her home and then picked up Connie in the DeSoto.

The 1958 DeSoto

It was two shades of blue: dark and royal. It had tail fins with three bullet-shaped lights sticking out, a big V-8 engine with push-button shifting, and it didn't like to cruise at less than 80 miles per hour. After taking me all across the United States — Florida, Georgia, Wisconsin, Rhode Island, California — that car traveled on a military ship to Hawaii. I felt like king of the road when I was behind the wheel. It was, however, beginning to show some wear and rust and could use some bodywork. The bumpers were a little rusty; there were some holes in the rocker panels; and some of the paint on the roof was fading.

After arriving in Hawaii, I took my new bride up to Diamond Head to look out across the Pacific, and parked at one of the lookouts. Next to us was a beat-up old brown Henry J, a car no longer in existence and deservedly so. The two guys driving it looked worse than the car and started to give us a big sales pitch on how they could transform the DeSoto, give it a bright and shiny new look. They would sand it, fill in the holes, paint it, even chrome the bumpers with a special paint that looked like chrome. They would do all of this for $500. And, best of all, they would finish it in less than a day and deliver it in the morning. In the meantime they would give us the Henry J to drive. I looked at my poor old car and said she deserved a bit of sprucing up. This was definitely in my budget. I gave them the keys and our address and took the Henry J.

Three hours later Connie and I decided we'd been taken and had just exchanged our car for a much worse one. I called the police. They were sympathetic but said the car was not stolen unless they did not bring it back when promised. They also said we sure had acted like suckers, since all we had was a name of their business. That was not much good, since we couldn't find it in the phonebook. All we could do was wait.

The next morning, right on schedule, they arrived with our beautiful new-looking car. It was a miracle. The chrome was shiny; the paint looked new; and the holes were all fixed. We were delighted and praised them for the work. I gave them a check, and they lamented the fact that no bank would cash a check to such a scuzzy-looking pair as them and asked if I would go with them to cash the check.

1958 Chrysler DeSoto

I drove with one of them in the DeSoto, and the other followed in the Henry J. We had driven about two blocks when there was a big bang: the transmission froze up and spilled fluid all over the street. I was furious and accused them of misusing the car and causing the transmission to fail, and I refused to pay them. They proclaimed their innocence and said they had not driven fast and that the car had been in the shop almost all of the time. I was so upset that I didn't listen and walked away to the nearest gas station, leaving them without the money.

At the gas station I bought a few cans of transmission stop-leak and more transmission fluid. I thought it might get me to a repair shop. I poured it in, and it worked. In fact the mechanic who checked the car said it might hold for quite a while and that it probably would have happened in a short time even if the car had not been run hard. Now I felt guilty, and Connie and I tried to find the men and give them their money. We even drove to Diamond Head to see if they were there. But we never found them. That was a happy story with a sad ending. We had trusted them, then distrusted them, then were delighted with them and trusted them, and then distrusted them again.

They never did anything wrong.

TOUR OF DUTY

The North Pacific in November

My title was assistant communication officer, and my battle station was on the bridge, handling communications. After only a few days of acclimating myself to the ship, the crew, and my department, we were off to sea and soon feeling the big swells from the trade winds as we rounded Kaena Point on the Western side of Oahu. It was quite a sight, as almost half the crew went to the rail to feed the fish. I have never suffered from seasickness but know that it is extremely unpleasant. It's critical that you get over it in the first 24 hours or it becomes dangerous; you can get severely dehydrated. When you first get seasick you feel like you're going to die; after 24 hours you're afraid you won't!

Several days later we were on station in early November on the northernmost 500-mile-diameter circle. Ice and snow covered the ship — quite a change from Hawaii. The waves were 15 to 20 feet high, and our little destroyer would rock and roll going downwind, then turn 180-degrees and go upwind. Our navigation was limited; with the overcast skies we couldn't get a fix from the sun, the moon, or stars. We relied on a very weak Loran signal and the best fix that the Willie Victors could give us.

On our third day on station the captain informed us that the barometer was dropping faster than he'd ever seen. Radio weather reports were not very accurate, but all indications were that a major storm was brewing. The captain sounded the general alarm, and we began buttoning up the ship. All watertight hatches were closed; all loose items were stowed away; the guns were locked in place; ammunition was stowed properly; and the ship was ready for the battle ahead.

When it came, it was like no other storm. It came fast, and it came furious. The waves began to build into small mountains at first, then large mountains. We had a boatswain's mate 3rd Class named Alua from Polynesia who was the best helmsman aboard. The helm was inside the pilothouse, which was closed off tightly with watertight doors. Outside of the pilothouse was the bridge, which was open on both wings.

The helmsman and the sailor who handled ringing the bells to the engine control room both stood inside the pilothouse. The captain, the executive officer, the operations officer, and I occupied the bridge.

We had a commanding view of the situation. It was scary. Huge waves were breaking over the bow, and the forward gun mount looked like it was loose and might slam into the Hedgehog antisubmarine weapon that was located just below the bridge windows. It was late afternoon and beginning to get quite dark when all of a sudden we looked out the bridge window and all we could see was green water. The bow was pointed down, and the entire stern was out of the water with the propellers shaking the back of the ship violently.

We looked up at this massive wall of water that was going to engulf the entire ship. The captain yelled at us to hit the deck and grab onto some piping. We got down on our hands and knees and grabbed anything we could find.

With a huge crash the wave came down upon us and completely filled the bridge with water. I stood up and was underwater; the fact that it was cold was of very little importance. The fact that I was completely underwater was of great importance. We could feel the ship rising: as it did, the water drained rapidly out of the bridge, and we were able to breathe again.

Alua held onto the helm and managed to keep the ship under control. The captain ordered damage control to give us a report as soon as possible. Our view from the bridge showed extensive damage to the forward three-inch gun mount. Amazingly, the stanchions from the bow to about a third of the way back were all laid back. These were three-inch steel pipes with cable running through them. The force that bent them must have been enormous.

The full damage-control report showed that the forward three-inch gun mount had come off its tracking and was laying askew of the deck but still fairly well connected to the deck. Our primary number-10 sea-search radar that was mounted on the mainmast at a height of about 110 feet was completely bent over and useless, and the air-search radar just below it was inoperable. The only radar that we had left was the height-finding radar mounted on the back part of the superstructure of the ship. It could be used for both sea and air search, but it wasn't very effective. We estimated that the wave had to be well over 80 feet high to have reached the number-10 radar at the top of the mast.

That wasn't the end of our problems. We'd come to the edge of our circle, and we needed to turn around and go back downwind. Alua picked the appropriate time and started to make the swing, but the waves were just too big, and the ship rolled over on its side, and the mainmast actually lay in the water.

At the time the captain and officers were in the wardroom trying to get a quick meal. The table was now at 90 degrees, and the captain was sitting on the wrong end of it. Every plate, fork, and knife, plus all the food, came crashing down upon him.

But after the noise of all the table clutter hitting the floor and the captain, there was immediate stillness. We all started to count under our breath. We knew that the ship had a nine-second period; that is, she would roll from side to side within nine seconds — if she were going to come back at all.

Six... Seven... Eight... Nine...

Here we got pretty worried.

Ten...

Eleven...

It was a few seconds later before she started to come back. Then, finally, she did what she was designed to do: right herself, even in a roll exceeding 110 degrees. Two men had broken bones when they'd been thrown about in the ship. But damage control reported that there was no life-threatening damage or any severe leaking.

It turned out that the *Forster* was the least damaged of all three ships on station and had to remain on station while the other two returned to Pearl Harbor for repairs. We stayed out for thirteen more days — during which time we had nine more storms. But nothing like the first storm.

During that time I got a real lesson in the life of a junior officer. Four of us had quarters in the after part of the ship right over one of the diesel fuel tanks. The vent for the tank was in our cabin. With each major roll, diesel fuel spilled out on to the floor. We were swimming in fuel, and the stench was sickening. Still, we had no choice but to lie in our bunks, keeping our clothes and shoes on top of us if we wanted to sleep. Fatigue was king, and we slept like babies in these sordid conditions. After thirteen days we'd fulfilled our mission and were relieved by other ships from the squadron. We headed back to Yokosuka, Japan, for some much-needed R&R and major repairs to the ship.

My first sortie was an experience I was not anxious to repeat.

Japanese Attack Pearl Harbor Again — This Time They Used Their Heads

It was 1964 and our ship had just returned to Pearl Harbor after our first six months of duty in Vietnam. We were berthed starboard side to Bravo Pier, one of the longest docks in the world. You could tie up a couple of cruisers, an aircraft carrier, a half-dozen destroyers, and probably a battleship at this pier. We were tied up near the shore side of the pier; behind us were two ships of our squadron. We'd just returned from a long tour of duty, so we only had a skeleton crew aboard the ship, and I was the duty officer of the day.

We hadn't been notified of any special events, but we did notice that far down at the other end of the pier, there was a band playing. Plus, a lot of brass was there to receive something. It all looked quite important. A few of us stood on the bridge to get a better view of the happenings. One of our crew that had just returned from shore told us that the occasion was the arrival of five Japanese destroyers, coming to Pearl Harbor to pay the first courtesy visit since World War II. This was going to be some show.

But we had no idea what part we were about to play in it.

Bravo Pier is situated such that the strong trade winds blow directly perpendicular to it. To dock a ship there, you come down the channel between the land and Ford Island, then make a right turn. Through this passage, you always have to take the wind into account: it'll push you rather severely onto the dock unless you have enough speed on to overcome it. The trick is to make a wide turn as you come around the corner. You need to come in fairly hot, then angle your bow toward the dock; at the last minute, just five to ten feet from the pier, you put a twist on to pull the stern in, go into reverse, and stop. From there, the wind will blow you gently into the dock.

Now knowing who our guests were going to be, we all stood anxiously on the bridge to watch for the arrival of the first ship. She soon appeared, making a tight turn around the corner of the dock. She was going slowly. Two hundred Japanese sailors were lined up on her starboard side in dress whites at parade rest. Far down at the other end of the dock, the U.S. band began to play. Our first thoughts were, "Uh oh, this looks like trouble. She'd better put the juice on if she wants to get out of this situation."

That was not happening.

A quick calculation showed that she would definitely miss our first ship, she might hit our second ship, but for sure she was going to hit my ship unless they put some JP-5 in the cylinders, and in a real hurry. I hit the general-quarters alarm, ordering the crew to secure the hatches and watertight doors.

"All hands stand by for collision."

Meanwhile, we heard the Japanese officers barking out commands and watched in amazement as all two hundred sailors put their arms out to fend off their ship. Our motor whaleboat, hanging out in davits, was the first casualty of this Japanese destroyer. Her sturdy oak frames were not strong enough to withstand a couple tons of moving ship. We could hear the crunch of oak frames breaking and screws popping out above the screaming commands of the Japanese captain. The next object the destroyer hit was about 400 hands extended out from the Japanese sailors who braced their feet and leaned their bodies forward to fend off. Another rough calculation: Each sailor would need to hold off about 10,000 pounds. They were not quite up to it, although it was not for lack of effort. As their arms bent from the force, the next point of contact was their heads, many of which took a rather severe blow. About half of the crew was knocked over on the deck. Next, the Japanese destroyer scraped down the side of our ship, adding a few more wrinkles and dents to our already battered topsides. Going into full reverse and twisting the stern out, she finally broke free and backed out into the main channel.

But this show wasn't over. Now the second ship was making its tight turn around the corner. They'd seen the carnage ahead and immediately turned left into the channel, almost hitting the first U.S. destroyer in the lineup, which had backed out into the channel. The following three Japanese destroyers all began to make maneuvers to avoid each other, our three ships, and the dock. Total chaos. The band stopped playing, and finally all the ships managed to line up and made a new approach to the dock, taking into account the force of the trade winds, and managed to secure themselves starboard-side-to without further incident.

We surveyed the damage — surprisingly minimal, except for the motor whaleboat and a few dents in the hull. My next action was to call the captain at home and inform him that indeed we were the first victim of the return of the Japanese to Pearl Harbor. He quickly returned to the ship; a short time later a small entourage appeared, walking down the dock. The captain of the Japanese destroyer was in full dress whites with his sword attached to his waist and gold braids adorning his uniform. One of his aides carried a beautiful little mahogany box, which contained a commemorative medal to celebrate the return of the Japanese Maritime Self-Defense Force to Pearl Harbor.

Hong Kong: Mary Sue

While en route to Vietnam, we were instructed to stop in Hong Kong to get the ship repainted. Immediately upon our arrival, while at anchor, a small Chinese woman named Mary Sue boarded the ship to negotiate the deal. She was all business and would only speak to the captain of the ship, no one else. As is typical in Chinese negotiation, she spoke loudly and could be heard by many negotiating her deal with the captain. I don't know how, but she knew highly sensitive and confidential information about where we had been and what we were carrying on board. She didn't work in cash, but bartered the paint job for our heavy-weather jackets we had for the North Pacific, the brass casings leftover from gunfire, and the leftover food to feed her team, and perhaps some of their families. We of course had extra security on board, but she left and came back with a crew of about 20 women, all dressed in the black pajama style/kung fu outfits to begin work. Using sanpans (little boats), they were efficient, fast, and no job was too big for them. They could do an aircraft carrier in a few weeks. They had us out of there in two days. It was almost comical to see this all-woman team, Mary Sue and her negotiating skills, and how fast they worked.

In Vietnam: Pranking the Russians

The Gulf of Tonkin incident occurred on August 2, 1964. The USS *Forster* was the third U.S. naval ship on station in Vietnam after that.

At the end of our second patrol on the Distant Early Warning line in the North Pacific, we were returning to Pearl Harbor when I received an encrypted message — Captain's Eyes Only. Since I was the Top Secret Control Officer, I, of course, also knew the contents of the message. The message came from CINCPACFLT (Commander in Chief Pacific Fleet) and directed us to return to Pearl for two weeks of refitting the ship for duty in the South China Sea. When we arrived in Pearl, a swarm of technicians descended upon the ship outfitting us with additional electronics including new electronic encrypting machines and electronic countermeasure machines. Having new crypto gear was a godsend to me, since the old system was manual and took hours to encrypt just a few messages. The crew was given maximum R&R, since our next trip was going to be a long one.

We departed Pearl in the spring of 1964, our orders directing us to Vietnam's east coast near the city of the Vung Tau. We were to be the first ship to intercept shipments of arms and supplies traveling from North Vietnam to South Vietnam by sea. The operation was code-named Market Time.

Upon arrival in the South China Sea, we were to rendezvous with one of the two U.S. destroyers already off the Vietnam coast. We arrived in the late afternoon and saw the destroyer ominously drifting in the bay. We were under radio silence and soon saw a flashing light asking our captain to please come over to the other destroyer. We lowered the motor whaleboat, and the captain left instructions to the executive officer to take command and bring the ship quietly to general quarters so that all crewmembers were at their battle stations and the ship was ready for action.

Shortly after the captain arrived on the other destroyer, Combat Information Center reported an unknown aircraft approaching us from a distance of about 25 miles and heading directly toward us. We were pretty nervous — we'd just arrived in the war zone and hadn't been in any combat situation. On the bridge were the executive officer, the operations officer, and I. My job was to handle communications. Our height-finding radar indicated that the plane was losing altitude and was only a few thousand feet above sea level.

We turned our three-inch guns in the general direction of the aircraft, and our spotters tried to locate it so that we could lock our radar onto the plane. The executive officer directed me to try to contact the plane. Utilizing the emergency frequency, I called out "Unknown aircraft: identify yourself" and continued to repeat this call a number of times. There was no reaction from the aircraft, which was now about three miles away. Finally I changed the message to "Unknown aircraft: identify yourself. Guns are locked on and tracking." Now we got some action as the plane peeled off and headed out to sea. Our spotters were able to see her quite clearly in their binoculars and identified her as a U.S. Navy propeller-driven plane.

One thing that was interesting was that the other destroyer did not have her guns manned until they heard our radio transmission and finally went to general quarters. Captain Campbell, our captain, reported the incident to command headquarters in Saigon and was livid about the incident, which was not very funny. It did, however, alert us to the fact that we were quite vulnerable and quite alone in the area. A previous attack on the other two destroyers had come from motor torpedo boats in the Gulf of Tonkin, stationed in Haiphong in the northern part of the Tonkin Gulf. We deliberated upon what we would do if one or more torpedo boats attacked us.

Our armament was not our strong point, since we were outfitted to look for planes and snoop on electronic transmissions. The *Forster* was equipped with two three-inch, rapid-fire, radar-directed guns mounted on turrets fore and aft. Above the forward guns was a weapon called a Hedgehog antisubmarine weapon, which fired a group of tube-shaped missiles in a circular pattern meant to explode upon contact with a submarine hull. We also had two torpedo launchers, which carried eight homing torpedoes. At the stern on the fantail of the ship we had two rows of the depth charges. Our guns were effective once they locked onto a target, but that wasn't easy to do.

The captain called all of the officers into the wardroom to discuss a plan of action in the event of a torpedo-boat attack. We formulated a unique plan in which we would set our depth charges at a very shallow depth, turning our stern toward the attacking boats, fire at them with our three-inch gun on the aft turret, and release depth charges, which would blow up several hundred yards behind the ship, running at full speed of about 19 knots.

This is how things often happened in Vietnam. We had to devise our own system of defense and offense, since much of this was new and not found in our tactical textbooks. Fortunately we never had to test our torpedo-boat defense system: the Navy brought a carrier group into the Tonkin Gulf, which quickly knocked out the torpedo boats in Haiphong. We all felt a lot more comfortable after that.

One night during our Market Time patrol, I had the conn, and the port lookout spotted a small fishing boat under sail. I asked the lookout what bearing the boat was at, and which direction it was going. We'd just received some of the first night-vision binoculars, so the lookout could see the boat, but we couldn't. The boat had no lights, and we were at "darken ship" condition.

He reported that it was going from right to left as best as he could tell. I asked him about how far the boat was from us and he said it was pretty close. I grabbed the glasses and took a quick look. Because of my sailing experience I could see that the boat was going the opposite direction and headed right into our path. I ordered left full rudder and full reverse. When the ship finally came to a stop, the fishing boat was not to be seen. I went out on the starboard wing of the bridge and saw that the boat was actually tucked under the flare of the bow, with several very wide and very white eyes staring up in great fear.

I called the captain, which was the normal procedure, to inform him that we had stopped a boat and requested permission to have the boarding party search the boat. He said fine and that he was coming out to take a look.

When he came out, he asked where the boat was, and I pointed straight down to the boat that was still neatly tucked into the side of our bow. The captain casually commented, "You're bringing them in a little close, aren't you, Olaf?" We didn't find anything suspicious on the fishing boat, but their eyes remained wide open, and I'm sure they kept their lights on from then on.

The Rocket That Got Us Into Trouble

Our Market Time patrols investigated all ships and boats that were within the 12-mile limit off the coast, and we took prisoners for interrogation if they did not have proper papers. We were to also confiscate any arms, food, and or supplies that looked like they were destined for North Vietnam. Most of the boats we intercepted were small fishing boats under sail or power. Occasionally a freighter or other large ship would venture inside the 12-mile zone and generally we would chase them out to sea.

The most frequent large ships that came near the 12-mile zone were Russian factory ships. A factory ship was a whale-processing vessel, but these ships did a lot more than cut up whales. They were bristling with antennas that were covered with canvas bags. All of this was electronic surveillance equipment used to intercept our communications and occasionally jam our radar. Once a factory ship was nearby, we would immediately proceed to it and run parallel to its course to prevent it from entering the 12-mile zone. We frequently would be alongside the ship for over an hour. During that time the crew of the factory ship was very busy taking photographs of our ship. They would stand on several decks clicking away with their cameras.

It occurred to me that we should use the opportunity to create a little confusion in the Russian spy system. I talked to my Snipes (engine men) and asked them if we could make a fake rocket with the materials that we had on board. We had quite a few 55-gallon oil drums and we had some sheet metal for the nosecone. They said it would be no problem. I then spoke to the captain, and he thought it was a great idea and encouraged us to go ahead.

We welded three drums together, formed a nose-cone, and welded a base to the lower drum, so that it would sit at about a 60-degree angle. We painted it white with blue "U.S.A." and some numbers on the side. There was a spot between the height-finding radar and the after gun mount that at one time had an antiaircraft gun mounted in it. We positioned the "rocket" there so that it angled aft, and we made sure that the base was well hidden. Our "rocket" was ready to launch.

Within days a factory ship showed up, and the fun began. We positioned ourselves a hundred yards away and paralleled her course. At first only a few crew were seen on deck with their cameras. Soon there were a dozen or more, then another dozen. We stayed alongside long enough to make sure they got enough pictures. It was an unlikely sight. The *Forster* was a pretty old ship and did not look like a guided-missile frigate. I am sure they pulled out Jane's Fighting Ships and scoured the pages to see if they could find anything like our ship with the big missile on the back. It was a lot of fun for a while.

About every two weeks we would be refueled at sea by a tanker with JP-5 diesel fuel. Tankers were deep-draft vessels and commanded by a full captain. The *Forster*, on the other hand, was commanded by a lieutenant commander, a full two ranks below a captain. Rank generally did not come into play during a refueling exercise. In fact, the ship with the best movies had the greatest bargaining power, and the two commanders would bicker back and forth over westerns and beach-bimbo movies with such stars as Elvis Presley and Annette Funicello. This exchange was done with telephone lines strung between the two ships along with fuel hoses and additional lines for transporting people and supplies across from one ship to the other.

Shortly after we had the encounter with the Russian factory ship, we were notified that a tanker would be rendezvousing with us. We still had the rocket mounted on the back of the ship. As soon as the telephone lines were hooked together, the tanker captain asked our Lieutenant Commander Campbell what in the devil was that on the back of our ship? Captain Campbell played coy and replied that it was classified with a need-to-know. The full captain was noticeably irritated at the reply. There was not a lot of discussion over movies.

About a week later we were to go into Subic Bay in the Philippines for a little R&R. When we entered Subic Bay a flashing light from a cruiser with the flag of COMCINCPACFLT commanded that the CO USS *Forster* report immediately to the Admiral. Captain Campbell looked pretty nervous. We lowered the motor whaleboat with the captain aboard even before we anchored.

About an hour later he returned and immediately went up to his cabin. A moment later the speakers blared out for Lieutenant Harken to report to the captain's cabin on the double. Now I was nervous. When I arrived, he chewed me up and down and told me to get that blasted rocket off the ship immediately. The Admiral had not been too impressed with the little Destroyer Escort Radar Picket Ship playing games with Russian spy ships.

It seems that shortly after we had been refueled, the tanker captain and the Admiral were having dinner together at the Officers' Club in Subic Bay. The Captain asked the Admiral what this little rocket was doing on the back of the *Forster*. He told the Admiral that the captain of the *Forster* refused to tell him what it was and what it was being used for. The Admiral, of course, didn't know anything about it — not something admirals are accustomed to. You can guess the rest. We still think it was a great prank and probably cost the Russians countless hours of trying to figure it out.

MEANWHILE, BACK IN MADISON

While I was in the North Pacific, fending off national incidents, Peter was tinkering with some pretty interesting projects back in Madison. The U.S. Army had contracted with Gilson Medical Electronics to build a cardio-encephalograph machine that medics could carry in the field. In those days, an 8-channel or 16-channel pen-activated EKG still used test tubes; they were the size of a refrigerator. Peter, alongside electrical experts, designed the mechanics of an EKG that could fit in a backpack. This had two consequences. For one, it placed him on a project the Army deemed "mission critical," so it kept Peter out of the draft in those early days of the Vietnam War. Of course, as soon as he finished the project, he was right back at the top of draft list; Peter eventually enlisted in the Army Reserves.

More significantly for the Harken brothers and our future, projects like these gave Peter and me access to Gilson's great machine shop.

We had both been getting more and more involved in competitive sailing and iceboating, crewing at the Mendota Yacht Club in 505s and other classes, and Peter's involvement deepened while I was off in the Pacific. One season he and Gary Jacobson acquired the bare hull — no deck, nothing on it — of an E-Scow, which they started outfitting themselves. As they did, they made improvements: opening up the deck, removing the rails, adding hiking angles and longer

E Scow: Ring Dang Do

tillers and hiking sticks. If the E-Scow class had allowed a trapeze, they would have added that, too. The *Ring Dang Do*, named for a dirty song that only a few people knew at first, was a platform of innovation. The song gained popularity after Peter's boat started winning races. The famous racing sailor Buddy Melges looked at the boat one day and said, "You know, if you dumb bastards really knew what you were doing, you'd beat everybody out there."

Let's just say our boat design was better than our sail handling.

Around that time Peter also found an Olympic-class Flying Dutchman, U.S. hull-number-one, in a junkyard. With a friend he spent one summer re-glassing it and fixing it up; now he had a trapeze boat.

All of these boats needed hardware: blocks, travelers, cam cleats. Lacking money, we had to scrounge what we could or make our own. In particular, the blocks on the boats we sailed at the club just didn't work well. Bronze blocks with bronze sheaves — they weren't near quick enough for the iceboating and the sailing we were doing. Big inland lakes usually have light air, so you need that light air to pull the sails out. But when the wind does blow up, then you need the power to haul those big sails in. In iceboating, there are lots of blocks between you and the sail: you need the parts to handle those loads. Well, with the blocks we were using, friction loss was near 10 percent. When you put six or seven or eight blocks in a series like that, then release the sheet, it doesn't even feel like it'll go out. With all that friction in the system, you have to push the sail out.

Peter started making his own blocks, using Gilson's machine shop in his off hours. At first, these were roller-bearing blocks, using steel needle bearings and rollers. They were better than the blocks with the bronze sheaves but still not great.

Then at one point in his day job Peter was designing a fraction collector: a machine with a round turntable that had a whole bunch of holes that fit test tubes in a spiral. Over these was a tube that would drop a measured amount of acidic fluid into each test tube. The whole table would rotate, ratcheting around to the next test tube. But because the acid was so strong, the table — which looked like a lazy Susan — could not use normal steel roller bearings; steel would corrode away in no time. And even stainless steel needed grease, which would have contaminated the samples in the tubes.

"I was really scratching my head," Peter said. "What are we going to use for bearings?"

Nobody used plastic ball bearings in those days, but he recalled that Honeywell used them for some of their vacuum and heating equipment. So he looked in Thomas Register and found nylon balls made by Orange Products in Orange, New Jersey — a company that's still alive today. He ordered several hundred.

"I cut a track in the aluminum turntable and mounted them," Peter said. "And, geez, it worked pretty nice. But when I was assembling, I had a bunch of these balls on the table, and they rolled off and hit the concrete floor."

Peter noticed how high they bounced.

"For some reason," he said, "my pea brain just thought, 'light weight, less mass.' These things might really work great in a sailboat pulley."

That night he sketched out the design for sheaves that would work with these nylon balls, then spent the next few days on the milling machines.

"They were pretty crude looking," he said. "But they worked pretty good, so we made sets for our own boats."

Soon, other Scow sailors noticed how easily *Ring Dang Do*'s boom and sails were going in and out without the crew moving around at all to push them. "They wondered what the hell we had, and we told them," Peter said. "They asked if we'd make them some, and we did. Of course, we lost our ass on every one because they were handmade."

But he'd gotten the attention of sailors like Buddy Melges and Peter Barrett and others who would reach the pinnacle of competitive sailing on an international stage. The success of gaining such interest really got Peter thinking of doing a larger-scale production with the ball-bearing hardware.

Peter Barrett and Lowell North, 1968 Olympic Games in Mexico

Chapter Five

Building Boats and Boat-Bits: Making a Name for Harken (1966–1968)

LOOKING FOR ENDLESS OPPORTUNITIES

My tour of duty with the U.S. Navy was up in the fall of 1966, and Connie and I went to Treasure Island under the Bay Bridge in San Francisco for decommissioning at the Navy base there. After driving to her home in South Bend, Indiana, I spent the next several months traveling around the country interviewing for jobs. I received offers from Lockheed in Sunnyvale, California, to be in charge of the wiring harness for the Polaris missile; from Ford Motor Company in Ann Arbor, Michigan, to join hundreds of other engineers in cubicles; and from Coca-Cola in New York to make sugar-water. None of the offers held much appeal for me.

Peter, too, had some great prospects, most notably a high position at Gilson Medical Electronics. "Doc," he told Dr. Gilson, "You know what my grades were like. You know what a screw-up I was through school. You know how long it took for me to graduate. Why? I don't deserve all this." But even in the face of Dr. Gilson's wonderful offer— Peter still wonders why he didn't take it— he saw a different future for himself. He'd started a small boatbuilding operation with a few partners, and now it was getting bigger. Instead of taking the solid job offer, he asked his little brother to invest in the company he'd started. One thing led to another, and I became a managing partner.

Our father couldn't believe it. "I think I've just raised the two biggest idiots on Earth," he said. After all the money he'd spent, all the crap we'd given him, he finally gets us through school, and now this. He knew the attrition rate of small start-up boat companies like this. All he could do was shake his head.

Scanda

Scanda started when Peter and some partners decided to build the Badger Tech dinghy. The University of Wisconsin had a fleet of MIT Tech dinghies, open-cockpit boats with just a rail on the side, for use as training boats. They were very tough all-around boats, but still the students were just pounding them to pieces. Peter had been a commodore of the sailing club, and the MIT Tech dinghies were in constant need of repair. Pintles were breaking; everything was breaking. "We can build a better mousetrap," he thought.

First of all, when the MIT Tech dinghies turned over, they'd fill up with water and you were sunk. Drawing on his experience sailing 505s and Flying Dutchmen, Peter thought, "Why don't we put in rolled-in tanks and make a self-rescuing deck?" In a horse barn out at Gilson Medical Electronics, he and a group of folks built a plug and a mold for the hull and deck for their new Badger Tech — "two horses, some old horseshit, and everything else: it smelled!"

Badger Tech Dinghy

They made the boats for the University of Wisconsin to slowly replace the open-cockpit boats. The boats worked pretty well — they were self-rescuing and they were more durable — which led to the idea of taking it further, to the Flying Junior.

Peter had several partners in that early operation, called Scanda. Peter Barrett — who won a silver medal in the Finn class in the 1964 Olympics and a gold in 1968 — had devised a method of gluing sails together and was in charge of producing the sails for the new boat design (the boats were sold complete with a set of sails). Scanda got its first order from the University of Wisconsin for 10 Badger Tech dinghies. Peter Barrett finished producing the 10 sets of sails for the boat order before he had to leave for the 1968 Olympic Games. Art Mitchel had left for Oscoda, Michigan to join the Air Force, where he was assigned to the Judge Advocate General Corps as a lawyer. Dr. Gilson had invested money into the fledgling company, but was not a working partner.

That left Peter Harken to get the job done. He needed more money, so he asked me to invest in the company with the promise that I would never have a better investment. Not having any place to put my earnings other than spending them as fast as I could when I went on leave or the ship was in a port, I sent in a few hundred dollars as a new stockholder in Scanda. After a long time and a lot of difficulty Peter was able to deliver the 10 boats to the university. Shortly after the boats had been sailing, a major problem developed with the sails. The glue that Barrett had used turned yellow and brittle and the sails soon fell apart. All new sails had to be made, which turned the black ink in the books to red, and left Peter Harken in a dilemma. He had no money left, and his partners were busy doing other things.

After I left the Navy, Peter asked me to come to Madison and join the Scanda operation. Peter still had a vision of making hardware utilizing the nylon

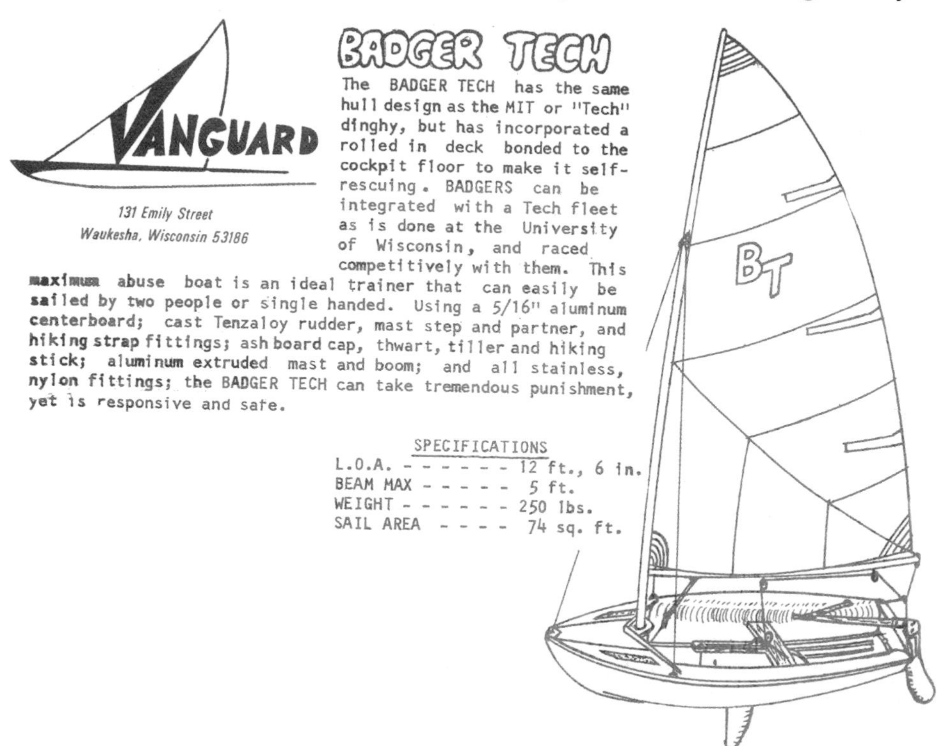

ball-bearing idea. The other partners did not want to give up the controlling interest and did not want to get into the hardware business. None of this sounded like a very attractive deal to me, since I was only offered a small percentage but would be taking a large risk. After Peter and I talked it over, we decided to form a new company — one that would build boats and also pursue his idea of making hardware utilizing the ball-bearing technology he'd developed. After going through many names, we decided on Vanguard — the lead ship in a flotilla of naval vessels. We wanted to be first in what we were doing, so we thought that was a good name.

We filled out our own incorporation papers in Madison, and without the aid of a lawyer we incorporated Vanguard in February 1967. Our next mission was to find a location. Peter decided that it was important that we get out of Madison and the influences of being in a university town. It was not a good manufacturing environment, and there were far too many distractions. Peter knew all of them.

We searched the papers in the Milwaukee and Waukesha areas and settled on a small shop on Emily Street in Waukesha that had previously been a machine shop. It was about the size of three garages, with a small office in the front and an overhead door in the back. There was a small stream behind the building from the Fox River spillway to give it that nautical flair. We rented it from two brothers who owned a machine shop called Riverside Mold and Die Company, which had outgrown their building. They were Al and LeRoy Stippich, and our acquaintance with them would play a big role in our future.

Delivering Boats to Cincinnati and Beyond

Our first job was to decide which boat we would build. The Tech Dinghy was popular at the University of Wisconsin but nowhere else except MIT. It only had one sail and looked like a little tub. The Flying Junior, a lively little 14-foot dinghy, was gaining popularity at other universities and looked like it was going to grow. It carried a jib and spinnaker to give the crew something to do.

One of our objectives was to build boats that could stand up to the abuse they would receive in a college environment. Nothing was available at the time, and the Flying Juniors in production were under strict international rules for international competition. We decided to build two versions: one for racing, and one for collegiate use. The "Club FJ," as we called the college version, did not exactly conform to the FJ class rule: it was built with extra fiberglass, a tough rub rail, and a stronger and simpler mast, rigging, rudder, and centerboard.

Club Flying Junior

So we set to work. In composite boatbuilding, you start by building a male "plug" in the shape and dimensions of your boat — one part for the hull, another part for the deck. Next, over that plug, you build a female mold. And using this mold you can lay up any number of individual boats, using layers of fiberglass and resin.

That was just what we did. For the plug, we started by building a frame, then fastening plywood sections, carefully shaped to the exact form of the 10 stations we had lofted from the plans. We then glued and screwed three-eighths-by-two-inch planks to the stations to form the hull shape. Squeezing copious amounts of filler into the cracks, we smoothed out the form. It quickly hardened and was ready for sanding. Days of sanding, with increasingly finer grit and gallons of water, finally made our plug ready for polishing and waxing. We sprayed a tooling gelcoat over the plug's mirror finish. When this hardened, we spent the next several days applying layers of fiberglass mat and resin to the plug.

When the fiberglass cured properly, we built a rigid frame around the outside of the new mold so that its shape would be held when it was pulled off the plug. Using compressed air and wooden wedges, we released the mold from the plug and lifted it with a chain hoist. Inside this new mold a hull was laid up to the exact laminate specifications of an actual boat.

Peter, Mac, and the traveling station wagon entourage

To build the deck mold, we started while the hull was still held firmly in the mold. After that, we made the mold in the same manner as the hull. Once the tooling was completed, we were ready to make boats.

Now we needed an order.

We got our first order from Ohio State University after telling them that our boats were self-righting and self-bailing. The order was for six boats at $600 each — a fortune for us. In order to do this, Peter and I drove all night to Cincinnati in our Chevy wagon. Peter drove, and I worked in the back typing up our first brochure. When we arrived in the morning, we went to the library to use the copy machine and made a dozen copies to give to the members of the club. Fortunately, they bought our sales pitch.

Now we had to figure out how to build and deliver them on time. We still had no money and no employees, so it was time to go to the bank and to hire a few employees.

When we delivered the first boats to Ohio State, we had never actually sailed one: we were late with the order and had not tested the self-bailing concept (water rolls out when righted) we had bragged about. They wanted to see it. We held our breath when we turned it over to demonstrate this feature to the full crowd of students and advisors watching. Peter and I sighed with relief when the boat did what it was supposed to do. Thank God it worked.

Adventures in Accounting

Peter and I had set up an account at Marine Bank in Waukesha soon after we set up our shop. We met the bank's president, Tom Prosser, a man we immediately liked. He asked us about our business and even came over to Emily Street to see the operation.

Now with the Ohio State order in hand, we returned to the bank to see Tom and ask for a $500 loan. He gave it to us without question and was delighted to hear that we had an order.

As the weeks went by, we needed more and more money to finish the order and to pay Tom and Terry. It was delightfully easy to get money from Prosser, and there was a strong mutual trust between us. As he told his colleagues, "They would dig ditches to pay us back."

A few months later I asked him for $10,000. By then we'd received several more contracts and needed operating capital. This was a different order of things. "Olaf," Prosser said, "I'm going to need to see a financial statement, since this has to be approved by the board." I went back to the office with a basic accounting manual that I'd bought at the local office-supply store and, from the very crude journal I kept, created a balance sheet and profit-and-loss statement over the next few days.

I brought these in to Tom. He looked them over and said, "I'm going to have to wing it. If I show these to the board, there's no chance for you to get a loan. Olaf, you're going to have to get a real accounting firm to do your books, and you better get somebody to take care of your daily records, or you're going to get in trouble very soon."

Tom Prosser got us the loan, and we got an accountant.

Several years later Tom got us a $100,000 loan that saved us from losing our company. It was an unusual banking arrangement and was built entirely on trust. I will never forget his words: "I'm going to have to wing it!" Not the kind of language you typically hear from a banker.

Rose: Our First Employee

Although we weren't making much money, business was starting to boom. We needed someone to take care of the records, follow up on the orders, answer the phone, and type out the proposals — a Girl Friday.

We put an ad in the paper, and the next day a cute little blonde was standing on the other side of the railroad tracks trying to figure out if this was really a business or if she'd made a mistake in jotting down the address. Still, she crossed the tracks, despite whatever misgivings she may have had, and I, all dressed up in a tweed jacket, conducted one of our company's first job interviews. Rose had already passed 75 percent of the interview: she had come, and she was cute. Besides that, she'd never missed one day of school in her entire four years of high school. I thought that was pretty impressive. It didn't matter much that she was a poor typist – that could come with a little practice. She accepted the job and stayed with us for 40 years, ultimately becoming a senior manager and an officer of the company.

Rose went on to be in charge of all the company's human-resources problems, dealing with the countless regulations and paperwork in that field that come from the new society we live in today. It certainly was a lot more fun just a mere 40 years ago. I don't think there was such a thing as an HR department back then, and I bet Rose often pined for the old days when common sense was our best regulator.

Rose in the early days

THE GLAMOROUS LIFE OF A BOATBUILDER

Our little shop on Emily Street in Waukesha was one of our homes in 1967. Connie and I had an apartment about five miles away, on Clark Street in Pewaukee. Peter had no home besides a cot at the shop, so most of the time he lived in the apartment with Connie, me, and Mac — Peter's dog and constant companion. We opened the shop between 8 and 9 a.m., took a midday lunch break, went back to work, opened a few beers around 5, went to dinner, and then usually returned to the shop around 8 p.m. The police would stop by at 10 p.m., after their shift, to share a beer and play with Mac. This was our routine for the

Mac building public relations

Our first shop on Emily Street in Waukesha, Wisconsin

first year. Connie came home from her job as a floor manager at Boston Store most nights to fix dinner for two guys who reeked of fiberglass and beer, and who then went back to the shop all evening.

After we got a few employees — Rose, Bob, and Don — the routine changed a little. We still ate lunch at George Webb's and the Nashota House, but we needed a lot more beer. Bob and Don and the guys put in long hours in the fiberglass shop, and their incentive to work overtime was beer.

Reminder: Don't Leave the Toilet Seat Up

I'm not sure if Connie left me because I always left the toilet seat up, because I was often still slopping fiberglass in a boat mold at 11 p.m. after a full day of work, or because she had to live in Pewaukee instead of New York or another exotic place. In retrospect, it wasn't surprising. This was not exactly the life she'd envisioned after years of globetrotting to exotic places and being the wife of a Navy officer. She had lived in Hawaii, Manila, Hong Kong, and Japan. In Manila she lived with my parents and was the social hit of the international community. But here, I was just a poor, smelly boatbuilder in Pewaukee, Wisconsin.

Whatever it was, I returned home to our small apartment one night to read a letter from Connie saying that she'd left and would be seeking a divorce. She went to Las Vegas and got her divorce, then went into the Peace Corps. For several years she stayed in Cameroon, West Africa. She had a degree in French, and that worked well in the French-speaking country.

I was devastated, but had learned that I knew nothing about women. Like most men, I still don't. However, we do understand that we are wrong almost all of the time and just need to accept that. And always remember to put the toilet seat down.

Bob, Don, and the Plastic Fantastics

Universities loved our boats. They loved the extra strength we offered over standard boats. And they especially loved the self-bailing cockpit. This simple feature, which is the norm today, gave us an edge over other boats at the time.

As the orders came in, our ability to produce lagged, and we subcontracted the fiberglass work with another company. The workmanship was not to our liking, so we decided to do it in-house, and placed an ad in the paper for an experienced fiberglass man. We were prepared to pay around $7 per hour for one man.

Prepping an FJ mold

Looking on while Bob Gramins works on an FJ assembly

The Plastic Fantastics (Bucketheads)

A few days later two men, Bob Gramins and Don Michelson, showed up. They said they were a team and would take the job for $10 per hour per man. They did not ask; they told us. Bob had a round face and balding hair and had a friendly arrogance that oozed self-confidence. We laughed and told them we could only afford one man at $7. Bob told us we could not afford to not have them. They would prove it, he said. He was an expert in glasswork, and Don was a mold-maker extraordinaire. They'd come in on Saturday, he said, and make a boat for us.

It was an offer we couldn't refuse. They came in as promised and immediately started to criticize just about everything they saw. Our molds were not properly waxed, our roller tools were bad, our patterns were no good, our laminate schedule was wrong, we were not catalyzing properly, and our gelcoat guns and procedures were a joke.

Peter and I were so mad that we considered throwing them out. But they just continued on: they rewaxed the molds, cut new patterns, and set up wetting tables. Then they started to work. And to see these two guys — it was like poetry in motion. Don gelcoated the molds while Bob prepared the work area. They wetted out the glass on tables and had it cut so that they could unroll it and it would fit almost perfectly to the next piece. No extra resin was pooled in the boat, and they rolled out the air bubbles with ease and speed.

They finished the hull in half the time it took us. And the final product was so much better! We couldn't believe it.

We made a deal. We told them we would pay what they asked. But they had to understand that if we lost money, they'd have to quit. Bob and Don were beer drinkers, and we always had cold beer on hand, since we needed some during the late hours. This was the added incentive they required, and we ended each day with a few cold beers. Sometimes more than a few.

As time went on, we hired more people in the laminating shop. Bob always wanted inexperienced men so he could train them from the start and not deal with bad habits. The team was so good that they became known as the Plastic Fantastics. Some of our other first employees, Terry Little and Tom Downing, were a little less knowledgeable about fiberglass than Peter and I but had a strong work ethic and good attitude. They did everything: fiberglassing, bonding the hull and deck, mounting fittings, rigging the mast, cleaning and polishing, and loading the boats on a trailer that we had built to carry six boats.

At our tiny little shop on Emily Street we were in production and ready to deliver our first order of boats. Vanguard entered the world of Olympic-class boats and became a dominant force in international sailing dinghies.

Entering the Olympic Classes

Bruce Kirby is a world-famous yacht designer whose most successful boat is the Laser, a simple and fast 14-foot, cat-rigged boat of which some 200,000 units have been built. It has also become an Olympic class. Bruce also designed the Canadian 12-Meter boat for the America's Cup, among a multitude of other designs. Before he got into designing, he was the chief editor of *One-Design & Offshore Yachtsman*, the precursor of *Sailing World*, and the premier magazine for racing sailors.

Peter and I went to Bruce Kirby's Chicago office to discuss the upcoming choice for a new two-person Olympic class. There were three boats in contention: the Strale from Germany; the Fireball from England; and the 470 from France. We wanted to build the chosen class. We were looking for a little help to figure out which boat it would be, so we could preempt the competition and get a license at a more reasonable cost. Looking at the different designs and the politics, we bet on the 470. It just plain looked better and was wildly successful in France, where they were building 3,000 to 4,000 per year.

Peter went to France and met with André Cornu, the 470's designer. He also asked Eric Marteau d'Autry, the manager of Dr. Gilson's office in France, to join them. Peter had become friends with Eric at Gilson's headquarters in Wisconsin. Eric was a big help; he was a businessman and could translate, since André did not speak English and Peter did not speak French.

Bruce Kirby, yacht designer and editor

Meanwhile, George O'Day, a well-known personality in the sailing business, was also trying to get the license, and it was going to be tough to beat him out. André looked at the map of the United States and determined it was three times the size of France. Since they were building 3,000-plus boats in France, he estimated we should build around 10,000 in the United States. Peter and Eric tried to explain that sailing was not as popular in the U.S. as it was in France, so that number might be a bit hard to achieve. André liked Peter and Eric and decided to go with Peter, who promised nothing except that we would do our best. It was lucky he did not ask to see the factory with the polyethylene spray booth.

At the International Yacht Racing Union council meeting in 1970, the members chose the new Olympic class. It was indeed the 470, and we were off and running: in those days, Olympic status meant a lot more than it does today in promoting a class.

Master mold-maker Don Michelson, with a little help from us, built the tooling for the new boat, and it was so much better than any we had seen or made before. This was real production tooling. We built the first boat, and at a tavern on Pewaukee Lake we launched it with Doug Drake, the president of the new USA 470 Association, aboard for its first sail. Doug loved it and bought boat number two. It was lighter and stiffer, and therefore faster, than the French Morin boat that was being imported by O'Day at the time. Doug raced a 470 competitively into his eighties. He owned a number of boats over the years, but his favorite was the original Vanguard.

In the early 1970s we built as many as five hundred 470s in one year. We had a dealer network spread out all over the country and began exporting to countries all over the world. The Vanguard 470 was soon the premier boat in the class, and teams from all over the world were visiting the plant and getting some customization done to their boats. We would load each boat with the best and latest equipment and layout, but sailors still wanted some minor modifications. It was a lot of fun. We met and made friends with many of the sailors, friendships that last to this day.

SAILBOAT HARDWARE: WHAT'S IN A NAME?

By the time the Vanguard operation was up and running, Peter had been making his own sailboat hardware for years. His blocks with the ball bearings inside them worked great; they were light and did not require lubrication. He even put ball bearings in the cam cleats. His fittings were admired by other sailors, but not available to anyone beyond a small circle of friends.

Scow and iceboat sailors understood the importance of being able to release lines quickly and without error. If you had an eight-part mainsheet system on an iceboat and it went into an uncontrollable hike on two planks, you needed to be able to release the mainsheet system instantaneously, as you could get seriously hurt if the boat turned over at the high speeds.

There was a very nice ball-bearing block made by a man named Sharpnack in Michigan. He had procured several barrels of Fafnir ball bearings made of stainless steel from the Air Force at almost no cost. He'd previously been a master sergeant in the procurement office, which helped. These blocks used aluminum

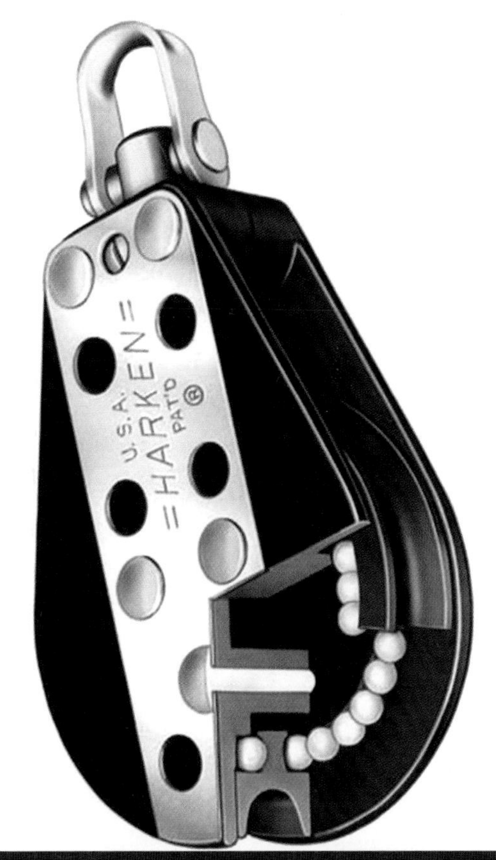

#001 The first production Harken Ball-Bearing Block.

sideplates and an aluminum sheave with the Fafnir ball bearings press-fitted in the sheave. They were nicely made and very popular with the iceboaters and scow sailors, but when the bearings ran out, production would stop, and there would be no more blocks.

#150 Cam Cleat still in production today. Peter was told it was crazy to put ball bearings in a cam cleat. More than a million have been sold.

Peter knew the value and need for the blocks and introduced the idea of producing them to his partners in the original firm, Scanda. Some of them did not see the need: it was expensive to make injection molds, and they didn't want to take the risk. After Vanguard had been formed, we decided to take some of our new blocks down to Chicago to visit our friend Gary Comer, who had a small hardware-distribution company called Lands' End. He also produced a catalog of sailing hardware, which was considered the bible of the industry. Gary literally handpicked every piece of hardware in the catalog. The editorial section featured a number of different boats with accurate drawings and photographs of how and where to use the hardware. He also described each piece of hardware as though it were a living entity. He had a knack for making something as dull as a hardware catalog into an entertaining and useful guide. Gary was also at the cutting edge of using computers. For such a small company, the room-sized Singer computer he had seemed incongruous. Most people now know that Gary's little operation turned into one of the largest direct merchants in the United States. In 2002 he sold his controlling interest in Lands' End to Sears for more than a billion dollars.

We brought a cigar box full of parts and a few blocks, and Gary was intrigued, telling us to hurry up and make them. He wanted to be our exclusive distributor. We had called them Vanguard blocks, but that day Gary Comer gave us an important piece of advice. We should put our family name on the hardware, he said; no competing boatbuilder would buy a Vanguard block.

And so the Harken brand was born.

Tribute photo of the Harken block as presented to Gary Comer in a cigar box.

Gary's offer to distribute our hardware was great news, but now we had to figure out how to pay for injection molds. That's where our landlords Al and LeRoy Stippich came into the Harken story. We had taken a liking to each other and had developed a mutual trust. Since they were tool-and-die makers, we told them of our dilemma. They said they would make the tools if they could also make the blocks. It was a done deal — one that lasted happily for decades. Part of LeRoy's humor was his grumbling every time we brought a new size and design to him. But, he would always come back with a beautiful prototype and product.

Some of the first blocks that Gary sold went to Buddy Friedrichs and Lowell North, who were headed for the 1968 Olympics in Mexico in the Dragon and Star classes respectively. They both won gold medals. This was incredible news to us, and of course we had to assume that the results were due to our blocks. Now we had to feed this line to the world, but once again we had no money. Back to Chicago, this time to meet with our old friend Bruce Kirby from *One-Design & Offshore Yachtsman* magazine. We asked Bruce if we could run a full-page ad and pay him sometime later. He agreed, but he wanted to try out some of these weird blocks. A few months later the magazine came out with our ad, but there was also an editorial describing the newfangled blocks that had almost made him lose control of his Star boat. The mainsheet had run out so fast that the boom had almost knocked him overboard. It was tongue-in-cheek, but many readers assumed the blocks were dangerous, which created more publicity. The overall result was very positive — with the great distribution through Lands' End, we had a winning combination. Harken blocks took off like they were on ball bearings.

Bob Stippich, 1986

LeRoy Stippich making our first injection-molded block components

It was a lucky convergence of many people — Doc Gilson (who first let Peter experiment on his milling machines and invested in the early business), Gary Comer, the Stippich Brothers, Buddy Friedrichs, Lowell North, and Bruce Kirby — all at the right moment to make it all happen. But mostly it was hard work and nice people who trusted each other.

Peter and I were not very smart, but we did know that success is linked directly to trust and treating people with dignity, and maybe a little sprinkling of humor.

Some of the first Harken catalogs

1968 Lands' End catalog with Harken blocks

Call us now - he won't be able to say that for long!

Bob Gramins - Sales Manager
and Art Mitchel - Director of Operations.

VANGUARD, INC.

1251 EAST WISCONSIN AVENUE
PEWAUKEE, WISCONSIN 53072 USA

TEL - 414-691-3320 TWX-910-260-3702
CABLE - HARKEN PEWAUKEE

CAM-MATIC® BALL BEARING CAMCLEAT

The Cam-Matic® is the most significant design contribution to sailboat hardware by Harken since we invented the thermoplastic ball bearing block. This cam cleat opens so easily, grips so hard and releases so easily, it could be considered almost fully automatic.

Why in the world would one put ball bearings in a cam cleat? That question has often been asked, and it's not because we have a mania for ball bearings. If a line with 100 lbs. goes through a cam cleat, each bearing does not have 50lbs. on it, but 171lbs. In other words, the load on the bearings is 70% more than the line load, and if there ever was a need for a good ball bearing system, this is it. Other benefits are: You can use a lighter spring, making opening even easier and the teeth do not need to be as sharp because the closing and squeezing action of the cam is not being counteracted by friction.

We did not stop at the bearing design, but looked at every aspect of the cam and designed a multitude of other features into it to make it really good. These features are shown on the drawing.

SPECIFICATIONS:

Hole spacing — 1½" (38 mm)
Supplied with 2 — #10 x 2" (5 mm x 51 mm) stainless F.H. screws
Overall length — 2 9/16" (65 mm)
Width — 1¼" (32 mm)
Overall Height — 1⅛" (28 mm)
Max. recommended working load 300 lbs. (136 kgs)
Breaking strength — 750 lbs. (340 kgs)
Line size — ⅛" (3 mm) to ½" (13 mm)

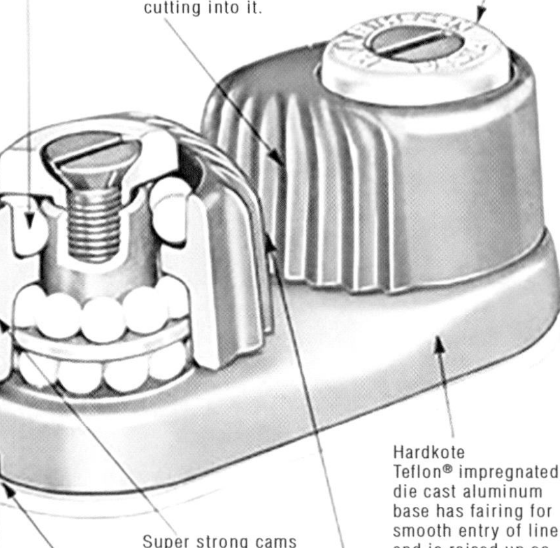

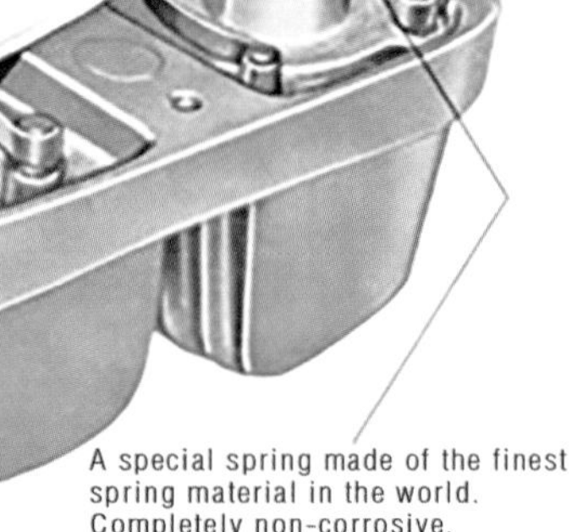

The Vanguard Olympic Finn – Selected by the Los Angeles Olympic Organizing Committee for use at the 1984 Olympic Games.

At a time when many Americans are driving Japenese cars, the Japanese are buying American small boats – Vanguards! This year Vanguard sold more small boats to Japan than Pewaukee residents imported cars from Japan! Vanguard also sold fleets of boats to Turkey, Venezuela, Greece, Yugoslavia, France, Malaysia, Mexico, Holland, Austria, Russia, Finland, and individual boats to Australia, New Zealand and Canada.

The strength of the U.S. dollar abroad has hurt foreign sales of some products, but foreign boat orders are strong at Vanguard – a real testament to the value of a Vanguard boat. When a sailor outside the U.S. is paying 30% more, he demands a quality product – there is no "buy American" sentiment overseas.

Vanguard makes the 470, Finn, Optimist Dinghy, Tech, 420, FJ, and Volant. If you want real value in a small boat, call us.

EXCELLENCE IS OUR STANDARD

1251 East Wisconsin Avenue, Pewaukee, Wisconsin (U.S.A.) 53072 • (414)691-3320 • TWX 910-260-3702

Chapter Six

Where In the World Is Pewaukee? (1968–1974 and Beyond)

EXPANDING

All Together on Elizabeth Street: North Sails Midwest, Vanguard, and Harken

Business was improving. The colleges liked our boats, and the orders were flowing in. It took a lot of selling and a lot of road trips. We showed up all around the Midwest with a two-boat trailer and another boat atop the roof of our station wagon. One day we got a call from the University of Texas sailing club asking if we could demonstrate our boats. We said sure, and packed three boats on the rig and began the long drive to Texas. It was about a 24-hour trip, and we finally arrived exhausted but ready to put on our show. The only problem was there was no one around. It was spring break; nobody knew anything about our promised demonstration.

"Sorry," they said. "Come back again."

Most of the trips were very fruitful, and we were busy cranking out Flying Juniors and delivering them as fast as we could build them. We needed more space.

Peter Barrett had moved to California to work for Lowell North after he and Lowell had sailed for a gold medal in the 1968 Olympics in the Star class. Lowell was establishing sail lofts in California and asked Peter to manage the one at Newport Beach. When Peter called Charlie Miller, another old UW-Madison

Rose with a batch of FJs at our Elizabeth Street building

buddy, Charlie's love for sailing got the better of him, and he left his well-paying job selling furniture in Mississippi. After several years both Peter and Charlie wanted to return to their native Wisconsin; they made an agreement with Lowell to establish a Midwest loft, North Sails Midwest.

Charlie came to see us, and it seemed natural for us to get together: we needed more space, and he needed a place to run a sail loft. After scouting around Waukesha, we found a large basement in an old food-distribution building on Elizabeth Street in Waukesha. The building had a number of tenants, including a photographic studio above us. We decided to split the space into a wooden floor area for the sail loft and a boat-assembly production area separated by a polyethylene wall that was "securely" fastened with a staple gun. We kept the fiberglass shop on Emily Street and transported the hulls and decks to Elizabeth Street, two miles away.

The arrangement worked great. We were now building 470s in addition to FJs, and the sail loft quickly became popular. We moved our office to Elizabeth Street, where Rose answered the North, Harken, and Vanguard phones, which kept her pretty busy in addition to filing orders, invoicing, bookkeeping, and secretarial functions.

Bill Joyce joined Charlie at the sail loft. The two of them had some unique methods of answering the phones when they were at their desks. If the Vanguard phone rang, the greeting would be "Hello, this is John J. Vanguard the Third. Can I help you?" You can imagine the confusion on the other end.

We had a lot of fun, even when things didn't go well. I'd made a deal with an RV camper company to provide them the extruded rubrail we used on our boats. They went through a lot of this stuff. One day I was in the back room where we did our shipping, packaging up the rolls, which gave us a clear $25 profit per roll. I was happily singing, "There goes another $25. And another, and another," as I put them in larger boxes. After shipping several thousand dollars' worth of rubrail over a few weeks, we anxiously waited for our money and subsequently found out our RV customer had gone bankrupt. The North and Vanguard group received no mercy, and the song "There goes another $25 out the window" became the popular hit of Elizabeth Street.

Building a Business, One Toilet Seat at a Time

One problem that we had early on was a visit by an inspector of the Occupational Safety and Health Administration. After looking at our manufacturing procedure, he was at a total loss about what to do. Our spray booth consisted of a polyethylene plastic curtain hung between the floor and the ceiling, with a $10 electric fan blowing the fumes out of the area. There probably wasn't one item or process in our shop that met all of OSHA's standards.

In despair, the inspector realized he had two choices: either shut the business down, or find some kind of a flaw that we could afford to fix to put in his report. He knew he couldn't let us pass. He checked our unisex toilet facility and, lo and behold, he discovered that our toilet seat did not conform: it was not split as was required for public bathrooms. He stated that we needed to replace it and that he would be back in two weeks to check on it.

We were trying to hold expenses down, so we fashioned a split seat out of plywood on our band saw and installed it. We hadn't done a very good job of sanding it or painting it, and Rose didn't like it. At first we thought we would change it back after the inspector had returned and finished his report, but he didn't show up in the next two weeks. After waiting another week, we decided to replace it with the old seat and keep the new one ready so we could make a quick change if we saw the inspector.

Sure enough, as soon as we had made the change, the inspector showed up and caught us with our seat down and not split. We showed him our plywood seat, and we all had a good laugh. He left shaking his head and fortunately never came back.

The Police Knew Mac by Name

Peter's dog, Mac, was the horniest dog I ever knew. If it was female and it moved, Mac was after it. And if it was in heat, there was no stopping him. Whenever the police heard there was a dog prowling around, they called us.

On one of the calls Mac was keeping the residents in their house, trying to look mean and snarling while he humped their dog. When we arrived, there were three squad cars at the scene, and this time we were warned that Mac was going to doggie jail if we didn't keep him under control.

Later, when we moved to Pewaukee, Mac managed to get into the basement of a house down the street where the owner kept two dogs that were both in heat. The owner came after him with a shotgun, but Mac managed to escape through a narrow basement window.

In another incident we had a lady from a house down the street demand payment to have Mac's unborn puppies aborted from her purebred.

Some years later, Peter and I went to a 470 regatta in Sandusky, Ohio. Mac was our official guard, and always stayed in the van or close by while we were sailing. Upon returning from one of the races, we discovered Mac had disappeared. An extensive search did not find him. After several days of looking everywhere and talking to the neighbors and the paper, there was an occasional sighting but no certainty. The newspaper

$100 REWARD

FOR INFORMATION LEADING TO THE RETURN OF

"MAC"

Mac is cross between a Labrador and Cocker Spaniel. He is all black with a white muzzel and white spot on his chest. He was lost at Sandusky Sailing Club on Saturday June 23rd and has been seen in the Port Clinton area on Thursday, June 28th. His owner was visiting from Wisconsin when Mac was lost.

Mac has been a close companion to his owner for over ten years and is very much wanted back.

If you see Mac, try and coax him into an area where he can be contained and call the Port Clinton sherriff at 734-4404 if you have him, or have seen him. He will not let you touch him and because he is frightened, may snap. He does have recent rabies shots and did have a brown leather collar on.

Please do help if you see him. His owner will remain in the area and will be available if you call.

REMEMBER: Call 734-4404 IF YOU SEE HIM

The missing-dog flyer for Mac

printed a picture of Mac on the front page. The calls started to come in, but still no Mac. I printed up flyers, while Peter kept up the search. We spread the flyers all over town, and one time even saw Mac on the other side of a railroad track. But a train came through and we lost sight of him. Finally there was a record of a black dog in the yard of a trucking company and Peter and Mac were finally reunited after almost 10 days.

Mac has long since passed and is in Peter's yard with a tree planted over him.

The First Pewaukee Building

Near the end of 1970 it was time for the companies to find more badly needed room. We found a pretty nice piece of property with a main building and two sheds in the town of Delafield overlooking the expressway. It was zoned commercial, and we made a deal with the owner and shook hands on it. When we went to sign the papers and give him the down payment, he reneged on the deal because the town fathers had threatened him that his landfill permit would not be renewed unless he sold the building to the town for a new town hall. It was one of our first lessons in doing business on a handshake. It didn't stop us from that kind of business, since most of the time we dealt with wonderful, honest people.

Our next venture was a piece of property again overlooking the expressway, on the Milton Morris farm. Milton badly needed the money since I-94 had cut

Harken, Vanguard, North Sails building in Pewaukee, Wisconsin

his farm in half. To us, it looked like an ideal site. But the neighbors didn't quite see it that way. They envisioned large smokestacks belching out black smoke and a big factory that was going to invade their country atmosphere. Emotions were so high that when we went to the town hall to watch and enter into the discussions, we decided to leave without identifying ourselves. There was no way we wanted to have neighbors who hated us.

Proud new owners of a mortgage

Today I totally agree with the neighbors. It was not a good place for a factory, even though we had made significant promises to keep the area pristine. We belonged in an industrial park, and that's where we went. The village of Pewaukee had just formed a new industrial park, and we were able to buy 4½ acres with sewer and water for $40,000. Today the price is 10 times that.

We needed more money to buy the land and build a factory. Peter, Charlie Miller, Peter Barrett, Lowell North, Roger Derusha (from Marinette Marine), and I all put in equal shares for the down payment, and we built an 8,000-square-foot building with the North Sails loft on one side and the Harken/Vanguard businesses on the other, and the offices in between.

We were now seriously in business and the proud owners of a mortgage.

Where in the World is Pewaukee?

So where is Pewaukee? To those who live here, it's the center of the sailing universe. It is located on the shores of Lake Pewaukee, about 20 miles inland from Lake Michigan and due west of Milwaukee — a good-size city with a nice mixture of the arts, sports, and a changing industrial base. Milwaukee used to be known as a blue-collar working city that had the stigma of the "Laverne and

Pewaukee Lake

Shirley" TV show of the 1970s hanging over it. Today it's peppered with smaller industrial businesses, such compelling architecture as the Calatrava-designed art museum, and a revived and bustling downtown. A little over a million people live in and around the city, and Chicago is only 90 minutes away.

Pewaukee sits on the edge of the Kettle Moraine, a hilly landscape carved out by a glacier, leaving ravines, hills, crevasses, and lakes. There are six fairly large lakes within 15 miles and many small lakes and ponds. Pewaukee Lake is the best sailing lake: it lies in the general east-west direction, the same as the prevailing winds. There are two distinct halves to the lake, with a peninsula called Rocky Point jutting out to delineate the two halves. The village of Pewaukee lies at the far end of the eastern half; its long, sandy beach is very popular in the summertime for its music, restaurants, waterski show and events. This is the fishing end of the lake, where the average depth is only 15 feet. We do all our sailing on the western end of the lake, where the depths range between 30 and 45 feet. The total length of the lake is 4½ miles, and the western end is close to 3 miles long and a mile wide.

The Pewaukee Yacht Club is located on the western end near Rocky Point. The competition is first-class and intense. The social life is superb, and the scows are exciting, high-performance boats, unique to the Midwest. For about six days of each week during the summer, the club runs races for around 160 boats: Optimists, X Boats ("Cub Boats"), Lasers, high-performance Melges 17 Scows, cat-rigged 16-foot MC-Scows, 20-foot cat-rigged C-Scows, sleek 28-foot E-Scows, and magnificent 38-foot A-Scows.

At Home in the Beach Park House: Ruth

I just mentioned two things that make me realize I'm getting ahead of myself again. Ruth.

It only took me about two minutes to make up my mind that I wanted to make a move on her. She was beautiful, and I think when our eyes met on that first night in 1970, I went straight over and said "hello" or something stupid. She didn't brush me off, which was one point in my favor. Soon we were having a nice conversation, and she actually seemed impressed that I was a boatbuilder. I too was impressed when she told me she was an auto mechanics teacher. She was actually an art teacher at Waukesha South High School, but had me going. She later told me that in her mind she had said to herself, "This is the man I'm going to marry."

Just when things were going well, a fight broke out, and I had to intervene because our friend (and business partner) had had too much to drink and had insulted the hostess. The hostess's boyfriend was a big brute, and he clobbered our friend. We had to take him to the hospital for a few stitches, but fortunately before we left I had gotten Ruth's address and phone number. I don't know why, but even though we were not too popular after we had crashed the party, insulted the hostess, and got into a fight, she accepted my request for a date.

Ruth, my beautiful wife, 1968

I tried to really impress her on our first date and took her to the "Pink Palace," an old dance hall and bowling alley on the shores of Pewaukee Lake. The big attraction there on Saturday nights was the Red Garter Girls, two middle-aged women dressed in fishnet stockings and short red dresses who sang, played accordion, guitar, and told risqué jokes. They were funny, and even if it was not a class act they did make us laugh. We had a lot of dates over the next two years. I knew I loved her, and she loved me, but I was reluctant to make a commitment after the failure of my first marriage.

Remember: Have Fun Along the Way

We had some great parties in those early years, but one at Coachlight Village, where Ruth used to live, stands out. Bill Joyce and Roger Wood ordered a crate full of lobsters that were flown in from Boston and put in our bathtub with a couple of bags of ice. We had a great big lobster boil with about 50 people showing up. The booze flowed freely and there were a lot of drunk people we did not want driving, so a lot of them stayed overnight. They slept everywhere: in chairs, under tables, on the floor, and in the bedrooms.

The next morning the place was a disaster. There were bodies and booze all over the floor and outside were the remains of a few dozen lobsters, which were beginning to smell pretty bad. One particularly bad experience was opening the freezer and seeing a poor old ice-encrusted lobster still moving around. Somehow he had missed the pot of boiling water and the only solution our impaired minds could think of was to put him in the freezer.

On Friday nights the ritual was to go to Dick Manhart's, a popular bar and restaurant that specialized in great martinis. We usually had too many but somehow managed to navigate ourselves back home. The drinking and driving laws were a lot more lenient in those days.

At one party a long way away on the northeastern side of Milwaukee, I managed to drink too much and asked Ruth to drive us back to Coachlight Village. At that time we all lived in the same apartment complex, but different buildings. I slept most of the way until Ruth decided to play a trick on me by pretending she was lost and needed directions. Little did I know that we were in front of our apartment buildings at the time. I looked out the window and began giving her elaborate directions, which she pretended to follow obediently; in fact, she managed to go in circles and ended up at my apartment again. I was very proud of myself for having given such good directions. She reminded me of this incident many times after that if I was drinking too much and asking her to drive. Ruth loved to play tricks on me like hiding in my closest and scaring me.

It backfired one time when I did not open the door and she spent an hour in the closet after I went to bed.

Getting Even

Four bachelors — including Peter and I — had rented a house on Pewaukee Lake that was a real find. It was a brick ranch, with plaster walls and ceiling that had been brought in from Milwaukee by two enterprising men named John and Lou. They bought 25 houses that were in the way of the new expressways for a dollar, moved them out to the country, and sold them for a huge profit.

John drove trucks for Borden's Milk and loved to sing gospel songs on his route. Lou owned a small restaurant on the south side of Milwaukee. They were about as unpretentious as a person could be. I bought the house with a hundred feet of waterfront in 1970 for $57,000. Today the waterfront alone goes for $10,000 per foot. We had a great house with a boat dock and had some great parties. The next-door neighbors had a great time watching the goings-on and the constant change of cars and people, while at the same time looking disapprovingly at our circus. We felt a natural, wild look was the easiest to maintain. We just let the grass grow and thought the dandelions looked nice in the tall grass.

In those days, when Ruth and I were first seeing each other, I was racing a 470 and often had Betty O'Rourke, the wife of one of my best friends, crew for me. We had the National Championships coming up, and at the last minute Betty learned she couldn't go. Ruth had some sailing experience but had never been in a high-performance dinghy with a trapeze. I was desperate, though, and asked her if she would crew for me. She reluctantly agreed, and we drove up to beautiful Leland, Michigan, near the top of Lake Michigan.

There was a large sand dune separating Lake Leelanau, a small inland lake, from Lake Michigan. The idea was to sail on Lake Michigan when the weather was favorable and the waves were reasonable. We would sail on Lake Leelanau during rougher weather. Somehow the race committee got it backwards. On the first day the wind was coming out of the southwest, and the waves had the entire length of Lake Michigan to build when the race committee sent us out on the big lake. As Ruth had never been on a trapeze before, I instructed her to grab the trapeze handle and hang out as far she could. I also told her that in the very unlikely chance that we would turn over, to hold onto the boat until I got it righted, and I would pull her in.

The starting gun went off, and all sixty 470s took off in the big swells and strong winds. I tacked onto port to get some clear air, and we made it through the first tack. Ruth had been hanging on to the trapeze handle and successfully shifted over to the other side, grabbing the handle on the port side. All of a sudden I saw a starboard-tack boat in the window of my sail and told Ruth we needed to tack now! I threw the helm over, but she wasn't quite capable of making it across the centerboard trunk in that split second. Over we went. After righting the boat I dragged her aboard and she was definitely not a happy person, so we headed for shore.

The next day the winds were light, so of course the race committee chose the small lake for racing. We needed to heel the boat over a little to maximize the waterline length, which meant Ruth had to sit on the uncomfortable centerboard trunk in the middle of the boat. I told her she had to sit on it, she told me "NO. I don't have to, and I won't do it." Ignoring my pleas as I pointed out that the other crews were doing it, she still refused. I sailed over to a pier and told her to get off. That was the last regatta we ever sailed in together. She told others later on that if I ever proposed to her she would accept and make me miserable for the rest of my life.

I finally bit the bullet and asked her father for her hand. She didn't know that when I got down on my knees and asked her to marry me. I even had a ring for her, and although it was not a very large diamond, it was the best I could do as a fledgling boatbuilder. She said yes more than 40 years ago, but it still seems like yesterday.

Ruth and I got married on December 22, 1973, at the Christ Lutheran Church in Oshkosh, Wisconsin. We had a lot of friends, and Ruth had a lot of relatives, so it was a pretty big wedding. Beautiful, too, and Ruth was a stunning bride. She cried a little and she had a sniffle, so I used my sleeve to wipe her nose. She hasn't forgiven me for that yet. I still want to know what else she could have done since I didn't have a handkerchief.

It was a winter wedding with snow on the ground and cold air, and to top it off it was next to the longest night of the year, which led to some joking. The church and the Pioneer Resort Hotel, where we had our reception, had Christmas decorations and lights and Christmas trees, making it all pretty special.

The reception was a blast, since most of the out-of-town guests stayed overnight. We had some great music and heavy hors d'oeuvres, so there was nonstop fun and lots of dancing. Ruth's mother, Trudy, even took a spill with good humor. It went on into the wee hours of the morning, and many of the guests ended up in the pool with all their clothes on, including the fancy dresses and tuxedos of the wedding party. Years later friends told us it was the most fun and best reception they'd ever been to.

To finish it off, we went to honeymoon in Las Vegas. I'd done a poor job of planning, as usual, so Vegas was one of the only options. It snowed there for the first time in 25 years, and the guys back home called to tell me the iceboating was fantastic. Of course, I thought they were giving me a hard time, but it was true.

Family Trip Down the Pacific Rim

When our girls were 2, 10 and 11, Ruth and I pulled them out of school for an educational, month-long business trip down the Pacific Rim. We went to Japan, Hong Kong, the Philippines, Australia, New Zealand and then planned a stop for R&R in Hawaii on the way home.

When I came home from work, the day before we had to leave, I walked in the front door to find Ruth had packed 17 bags for her and the girls! I am sure I lost my temper, but told her they were going to have to cut it down, or she and the kids would have to carry it themselves. Ruth was furious with me, and explained she had to bring enough diapers, casual and dress clothes, as well as summer and winter clothes for the northern and summer hemispheres, toys to keep the kids busy and things for Christmas. I'm sure she was convinced she wouldn't be able to get the same diapers overseas. She eventually got it down to 14 bags.

When we arrived in Japan and got through customs, Ruth motioned for a porter to come help us. She was about to pick a few bags up, but the man signaled for her to back away. He pulled out a leather strap, wove it through all the handles and picked up all 14 bags by himself. Ruth looked at me and said "Humph!" He looked like a brick. All you could see was a moving mass of luggage with two little feet walking under it all. He carried them down the stairs and out to the car.

Tad Ikami, our distributor, was waiting to pick us up. He saw the amount of luggage and was speechless. Tad had a mid-size sedan big enough for the family, but not the bags. So Ruth and I split up and hired a separate taxi for the luggage to follow behind us.

Years later, Peter and Göran went to Japan. Preempting how he thought Americans travelled, Tad hired a large truck to pick them up, but Peter and Göran only had one bag each, which left Tad completely confused.

Christmas in Australia

Our great network of distributors and business contacts makes it fun and relatively easy to travel without much planning. They usually plan something nice or fun for us and a place to stay — when we did the trip down the Pacific Rim, it was no exception. We planned to spend Christmas in Perth at the Lissimans' house during the 1987 America's Cup. John Bertrand was the winning skipper of *Australia II* in the 1983 America's Cup, ending the 132-year winning streak from the Americans. Skip is a good friend and let us use their home while they were busy with the Cup. He was part of the crew on *Australia II*. Our Australian distributor was in Sydney, so we were on our own for the most part in Perth. On Christmas day, people haul their Christmas trees down to the beach and stick them in the sand — decorations and all. We thought it would be fun to take the girls down for Christmas on the beach. Shortly after we got down there, the beach got more crowded. And it didn't take long to realize we picked the wrong beach — the topless beach. We tried not to make a big deal in front of the girls, but told them we should get back to the house to open Christmas presents. So the next time we did a beach trip with the kids, Ruth made sure to ask which beaches were kid friendly.

Sailing with the kids in Sydney, Australia

The Girl from Oshkosh — Flying Capital of the World

Ruth was born in Oshkosh, raised in Oshkosh, attended the Oshkosh campus of the University of Wisconsin, and was even a runner-up in the Miss Oshkosh Pageant. As I mentioned, one of our stops on the Pacific Rim trip was in Australia.

Heidi in the pilot seat of the 737 between Perth and Sydney

As we were flying across Australia from Perth to Sydney, the pilot announced that the kids were welcome to come to the cockpit. Heather and Heidi went up and stayed longer than any of the other children. We went to check on them. Heidi was in the pilot seat and Heather was in the navigator's seat. All of them were chatting away and having a great time. When we were close to landing, the stewardess came back and asked if we would please come to the cockpit. It turned out that the girls had said Mom was from Oshkosh.

For those who don't know, Oshkosh is the home of the Experimental Aircraft Association, or the EAA. Each year they have a huge event called the Fly-In, where over 7,000 general aviation planes fly in and park on hundreds of acres of land. The lines of planes are beyond belief, and it is the mecca for pilots no matter what they fly. Experimental planes are the focus, and the attendance rules are that they have to fly in, no matter how weird they are. There are War Birds, stunt planes and shows, big tents full of airplane equipment and building materials, and a star attraction like the Concord. For a week it is the busiest airport in the world. Our 737 pilot, born and raised in Australia, had been there many times and was delighted to have a true Oshkosh girl aboard. The girls even got to sit in the pilot's seat to hold the yoke and stay in the cockpit for the landing. It's hard to believe that nowadays.

Ruth with Heidi, Hilary, and Heather in Hawaii

Many people have no idea where Oshkosh is, and Ruth would hardly mention where she was from. After the Aussie incident, she proudly tells it and that it is the home of the EAA and Oshkosh B'Gosh.

Ruth lived at home during her college years and graduated from UW-Oshkosh with a B.S. degree in Art Education and had a second major in art. She later taught art in De Pere, Wisconsin. That was a real challenge since there was no budget for art classes, and most of the money was channeled into sports. Then she had an opportunity to teach at a much larger high school, Waukesha South, where they had a very progressive art department. In one of her classes she called the students her roller-derby girls, since they were all a little on the rough side, but she managed to channel their anger and frustration into good art.

Ruth eventually gave up teaching at Waukesha South to raise our three girls. This was a much larger project than teaching any art class and she did a wonderful job, but she loved teaching art and to this day is heavily involved in art projects, art organizations, and running school art shows.

One of her biggest projects was to commission artist Joel Pfeiffer to do a large clay wall for Pewaukee Public Library, which involved over a thousand people helping to stomp the clay and form it into tiles. Kids and adults in the community all took part in creating designs in the clay. The forms were then taken to the artist's home to be fired and glazed in his large kiln. The squares were reassembled in the brand-new library in the village of Pewaukee. Today there's a huge wall with this beautiful ceramic mosaic covering one of the walls by the stairs. She later repeated the project for the opening of our new building in Pewaukee; stomped and carved by the employees, it is on display in the main entrance.

Tom the Turkey

Michael's House of Prime is a nice steak house across from the Pewaukee Yacht Club that features great prime rib. A wonderful woman named Dorothy owned and managed the restaurant until she passed away. For a few years, they would host a Halloween party for her regular customers with prizes for the best (or worst) costumes. One year they had a western theme. Ruth and I had not done any planning, so at the last minute, we went to the local costume store. It was pretty late on Halloween, and they had nothing left in stock except mismatched pieces of a cowboy and dance-hall girl costume. The cowboy suit had rhinestones on it, a torn sleeve, and no hat or boots, so I used my Docksiders and a straw hat. Ruth had fishnet stockings with holes in them and a hat with feathers. We looked ridiculous among the others who'd labored over some really neat costumes. The judges, however, decided that we looked so stupid that we were awarded first place.

The prizes were a goose for third place, a hen turkey for second, and for first prize, a very large and very alive tom turkey. He was, according to our hosts, hand raised and not dangerous. I fit him in the back of our station wagon and brought him home.

The girls were only five and six so we had a fenced-in area for them to play. I took Tom out of the car, put him in there, and went to bed. Early the next morning Heather came running in our room and said it sounded like there was a laughing dog in the yard. We went to the kitchen window with the girls and they couldn't believe it. Tom spread out his tail feathers, exposed his wattles, and strutted about the yard.

Tom's next introduction was to Rachel, our black Labrador. We let her out and as soon as she saw the bird, she ran to attack. Tom tried to fly, but there wasn't enough room for a takeoff so he ran and flapped his wings in hysteria. Rachel got about 10 feet, but put the brakes on when she got close enough to see how big Tom was, then took off in the other direction. They soon learned to tolerate each other but were not fast friends.

Tom made it through Thanksgiving. He lived in a cardboard box on the porch and could look in the kitchen window. He didn't like me because I had to carry him, and he didn't like to be picked up. Or perhaps it was because he was in love with Ruth. Whenever he saw her, he changed his body from a sleek bird to the typical turkey you see in pictures with the tail feathers fanned out and the wattles under his chin dropping down almost to the floor. He would gobble constantly while he strutted back and forth in front of the kitchen window when Ruth was at the sink.

Tom also liked kids, and we brought him to Heather and Heidi's school for show-and-tell. He ran around the schoolyard with the kids chasing him. The superintendent for the school district happened to stop by that day and almost had a bird herself when she saw the kids with Tom, thinking all turkeys were liability threats. After meeting Tom, she calmed down and all was okay, but we were told it was time to take Tom home.

At Christmas he would come out of his box and scare the slightly inebriated neighbors who came to sing Christmas carols and have a wee drink. When this huge bird appeared out of his box gobbling away they started to run, but we told them Tom just wanted to join the choir. After a little more "eggnog" they agreed.

Tom went to a farm when he was too tough to eat and was seen herding cows. He also shunned the advances of a widow turkey, but finally a romance blossomed, and they had a rafter of little turklets.

You Load Sixteen Tons — And Déjà Vu All Over Again

Ever since my high-school days in the Mindoro iron mines, I've always liked heavy earthmoving equipment, especially the one that combines a backhoe with an end-loader. Ruth asked me what I'd do if I got one. My reply was that I would dig holes in the yard and then fill them back up. I never got one, but I did get to use one at our yacht club. We needed to move a large concrete slab in our launch ramp. A friend, Skeeter Johnson, had one and agreed to let me use it. The brakes didn't work, so he said I should be extra careful. He lived on a hill about a mile away, so it was an exciting and scary ride to the club, but I made it without incident.

I'd used the backhoe to gently nudge the slab into the lake when the whole machine began to roll down the ramp. I quickly jammed down the hoe, which had teeth in it. But apparently I'd pushed the lever a little too hard: now the bucket curled up so it was sliding on the smooth part — and I sledded right into the lake with no brakes to stop me. Next thing I knew, I was up to my chest in the water, and only the exhaust pipe of the machine remained above water. I swear half the club members were watching and rolling with laughter. I had to admit it was pretty funny. The engine ran for about 10 seconds underwater. We pulled it out with a truck and dried it out, sprayed out the cylinders with oil, dried out the distributor, and started her up. She ran like a top. I kidded with Skeeter that I felt she just needed a thorough washing.

Keeping It Fun in the Suburbs

Our nearest neighbors were Dick and Betty Schneider, wonderful people. Dick was our family dentist, and Betty was quite interested in being a good attentive neighbor. She was ripe for a setup, and I took advantage of that. One day I was putting up a makeshift zip line between two trees about a hundred feet apart by attaching a bosun's chair to a block. This was for the kids and it was well used for many years. When Betty saw me tying it to the trees she couldn't contain herself and came out to find out what was going on. She asked me what I was doing and I explained that I was putting up a laundry rope so Ruth could hang out the laundry in the sun. Mind you, this was in the front yard and visible to all. Betty was taken aback and stammered that she had a large group of ladies coming over from the Service Club the next day. This was great and I played it to the fullest, saying Ruth had all this wet laundry to bring out and it should be dry by tomorrow. When she was about ready to faint I let her in on the project.

When Ruth and I took over the house we had to adjust to a new life of being suburbanites and overcome the reputation of our house. We started to inspect what the neighbors were doing. On weekends they cut grass and killed dandelions and tended their gardens, where they grew vegetables and corn and herbs. We cut our grass and killed dandelions and decided to plant a garden.

I plotted out a piece of land on the south side of the house near a small wooded area. I thought a nice big plot would do well and Ruth wanted it about 30 feet by 10 feet. I got a shovel to turn the ground over and started to dig. The shovel went in about two inches and hit a rock or something solid. I moved a few paces and tried again. This time I managed to get in about three inches. Things did not improve, so I got out the pickaxe and started pounding away. After an hour I managed to turn about one square foot of the land. I quit and went in to talk to Ruth and come up with a new strategy for the next week.

We decided that the first thing to do was to decrease the size of the plot, so I reduced it to 10 by 20 feet. We also decided the ground was too dry and hard, so I got out the hose and started to water it down. I left the hose on for a few hours to make sure we got it really soft. I succeeded and created a quagmire — you could have slopped hogs in that pit. Another setback, and another week lost. We were already a few weeks behind the neighbors, and the planting season was coming to an end in a couple of weeks.

The next plan was brilliant. I got the car out and backed it up to the edge of the garden, tied a rope to the boat hitch, and tied the other end to the pickaxe. This was the old horse-and-plow method, using a car and pickaxe. Ruth got in the car and drove it down toward the lake, while I wrestled with the pick, trying to hold it upright between my legs. We went back and forth a few times while the neighbors were now starting to watch this program. You could almost hear the buzz of their comments.

Once again the plan failed since there was no way to hold the pick up straight. What to do next? How did the others do it? I was certainly not going to stoop so low as to ask them. Fortunately, as I drove by the local lawn-and-garden store I decided to stop in and ask them. Rototiller? So that's how it was done.

I rented a nice big one, since I needed to get the job done fast. I proudly showed the new toy to Ruth, and she came out to watch. A couple of pulls on the engine, and it roared to life. I started at the high side of the plot going downhill toward the lake. Releasing the clutch, the rototiller's big tines dug in and started to pull me and the machine through the garden and across the lawn toward the lake. I dug my heels in, clamped on the brake, releasing the clutch, and stopped just a few feet from the lake. I had only succeeded in making a big furrow across the freshly cut lawn.

Ruth looked at the machine and asked what the little spike gadget was on the back of the machine. It looked adjustable too. Well, we finally figured it all out and put the back tines down to control the machine by simply raising the handle bars up and down. It had taken three weeks to plow the garden, but we made the season and started to see the results with fresh tomatoes, peas, beans, and corn. The only problem was the rabbits were eating it faster than we could. We planted a separate garden for them, but they preferred ours, so we switched with them the first year. We were now real suburbanites.

Harken Observatory in Pewaukee — A Celestial Viewing Mecca?

While doing night watches on the bridge in the Navy, I would look up at the sky in awe. When out at sea without any light pollution, the sky is ablaze with stars. It became a fascination for me and later a hobby. At the time, our family was pretty crowded in our house. Our youngest was sleeping in our room and our two older girls were sharing a room. We needed more space for our growing family. I decided when we remodeled our house that it was a perfect time to explore my fascination by putting an observatory on top, and added it to the construction plans.

Of course I had to test different uses for our ball-bearing equipment and designed the observatory to rotate on Harken tracks and traveler cars. We built a special anti-vibration floor by putting plywood over four inches of sand and covering it with a rubber roof. The circular structure has a slanted elliptical acrylic top made of three panels; the middle one slides open for viewing. I installed a 10" Meade reflector telescope, with which I could see the rings around Saturn. From the pulley ride in the front yard between the trees, to my observatory, this was another one of my projects that had the neighbors talking and wondering what the thing was on top of our house. When I told them it was an

Checking out the new telescope in the Harken Observatory at Pewaukee Library

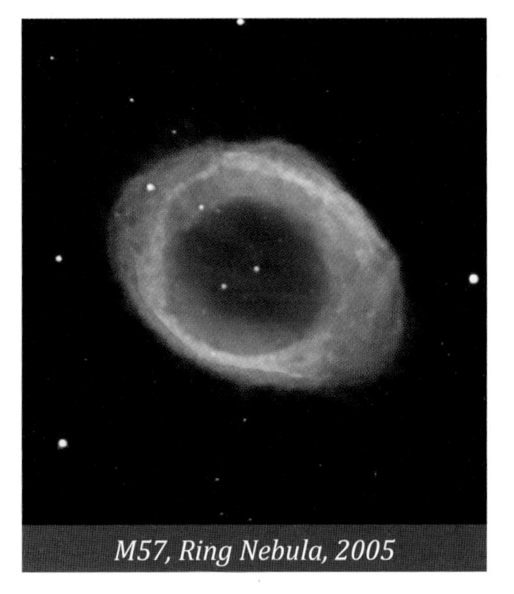
M57, Ring Nebula, 2005

M51, Whirlpool Galaxy, 2005

observatory with a powerful telescope, they would nervously joke about where I would point it at night. I am sure they were worried I was spying on them, but I would joke back that there were too many trees to see in their bedroom window.

I subscribed to astronomy magazines and kept abreast of all the latest stargazing events. I would take our daughters up and wait to see the space station cruise by, look for comets, the moons around Jupiter, the rings around Saturn, and go over the names of the craters on the moon. It was a fun hobby for me, but after sharing it with my girls, I had a desire to make this experience available to more people.

My experimental boat project, *Procyon* (later mentioned in chapter 8), was named after my passion — I liked the name of the star (actually it's a binary star system). Procyon is the brightest star in the constellation Canis Minor, and the eighth brightest star in the night sky. It is also one of the vertices of the winter triangle with Sirius and Betelgeuse. Sirius is the brightest star in the sky, so once you locate Sirius, Procyon is easy to find.

M42, Orion Nebula, 2005

Many years later, some land opened up in the village of Pewaukee. My wife, a member of the library foundation, and I joined a project to lobby and raise funding to build a public library in the town center to replace the tiny library that was too small to service the community. In looking at the plans, the sound structure got me thinking that this would be a perfect place to share something I treasured with the rest of the community. So we donated the funds and resources to the library to build an observatory on top, a truly unique experience for our community to have.

We bought a commercial dome system from Australia which had some great features at a price better than what we could custom build. That would allow us to put more money towards equipment. The dome rolls on wheels and is run by a motor that can be controlled by computer, a push-button control, or operated manually. This would allow us to lock onto an object with the computer and drive the telescope and dome into position to track the object in the moving sky. We donated a 12" Meade reflector telescope, CCD cameras, computers, a projector and screen system for viewings in the community room, and the funds to keep things running. The room and observatory are used for special events at the library, as well as special celestial events. I eventually formed the Pewaukee Astronomy Club after meeting local amateur astronomers and enthusiasts that were much more technical than I am to run the equipment and hold monthly viewings for the community.

The town center is not an ideal location to set up a telescope, but it is close and easy for people to get to with their families. In spite of the light pollution, we have been very pleased with the images we are getting with the highly sensitive CCD camera. Whenever I am able, I go to the weekly Astronomy Club meetings and try to keep it active in hopes to inspire young enthusiasts, bring together families, and make sure things are running smoothly.

Chapter Seven

Harken in the Wider World (1971–1991 and Beyond)

BOAT SHOW ESCAPADES

Boat shows are an important part of life in the marine industry, a chance to leave the shop and mingle with customers, colleagues, and competitors. In the 1950s and '60s, the indoor New York Boat show was the biggest of these. We went just once — and once was enough.

We were too poor to pay for the booth by ourselves, so we teamed up with Bruce Kirby and Ian Bruce, the designer and builder of the hot new little class called the Laser. We towed our 470 to the show and carried a block display. At that time, the show organizers wouldn't allow us to touch the boat or the display. The union controlled everything. Six big brutes were assigned to us to carry our 250-pound boat. They grunted and grumbled like it was going to be made of lead and almost launched it into space — it was much lighter than they expected.

We had to pay for everything. It cost $50 to get our one electric sign plugged into the receptacle by a qualified electrician. When the show ended, it took us six hours to get the boats out of the building. Our six brutes would not move the boat unless we bribed them with at least $20 each. We did not have enough money to afford this and still get home. So they did other jobs for those who paid their bribes, and they rode the freight elevator for hours looking for other work. In between jobs they'd go to the local bar and drink.

We complained to the floor boss, who let us know that he had no control over them. Finally I decided to ride with them and stayed on the elevator for a couple of hours. They were pretty abusive but finally moved the boat out after six hours of waiting. During the show packs of kids would run into the stand and steal as much as they could from the block display. We swore we'd never go back to that show again and never did. It was the beginning of the demise of the New York show. Almost a third of the exhibitors declined to sign up for the next show.

We did have some great memories from the show. Like the rest of us, one of our comrades had a wee bit too much to drink and asked a taxi driver to take him home. When the cabbie asked for the address, he told him his address in Chicago. The driver said the only way he could get there was to take him to the airport, which he did. Somehow our friend bought a ticket and was halfway across Ohio before he figured out what happened. After landing, he bought a return ticket and was at the show the next morning. The next night he locked himself out of his room after a shower and ran around with just a towel. Annapolis is our version of Vegas — many fun, wild and crazy memories were made there.

Annapolis

The United States Sailboat Show in Annapolis, Maryland — the first major in-the-water show and known among sailors simply as "the Annapolis show" — was the brainchild of Jerry Wood in 1971. It made a lot more sense than an indoor show: it cost a fraction

Olaf, Don Macaulay, and Peter circa 1994

of the New York show for the bigger boats, and the land displays were sheltered in large circus-type tents alongside Spa Creek, a tributary of the Chesapeake.

Our experience at New York had made us a bit skeptical of boat shows in general, and we decided not to display at the first Annapolis show but just see what it was like. It was a huge success, and quickly became a major gathering spot for sailors. The exhibitors loved it, too. We were all together in a small town, instead of being spread all over New York. The show was not only good for business but a lot of fun. It was the breeding ground for many good times — and some legendary escapades.

Here's the sort of thing that would never happen in New York. For many years in the Eastport neighborhood across Spa Creek in Annapolis, there was a sailor's bar called Marmaduke's. Publisher Knowles Pittman, whose reputation had preceded him from the New York show; Bob Bavier, the distinguished publisher of *Yachting* magazine; and Don Macaulay, the publisher of *Sail* magazine, were loosening their tongues over a "block" of martinis while discussing the merits of their magazines and the faults of the others. As the friendly banter continued into the late hours of the night, they almost simultaneously passed out. It was a sight to behold, and, believe me, the three icons of the sailing publications drew a crowd. Yes, Annapolis was the right town for convening sailors.

We decided to go to the second Annapolis show in full force. We got an outside land space for the boats and a tent space for the hardware. With our Pontiac station wagon, we trailered a 470, a Flying Junior, and a 420, plus a big hardware display. Peter's dog, Mac, was traveling with us, as he did on every trip. When we arrived, we were surprised to find all the displays of other exhibitors up and people already in the show.

We had the wrong date.

Of course, we were the butt of much kidding by our compatriots as we struggled to put up a display and unload all of the boats in the middle of a crowded show very much in progress. The management was not too pleased.

The next year we got the dates right, and off we went with our three-boat trailer, our Pontiac wagon, and Mac. We got as far as Gary, Indiana, when the transmission crapped out. We were able to limp along to a Holiday Inn in a very rough neighborhood. Peter and Mac stayed in the car to guard the boats and everything else. It was a scary night and a few times there were young men outside trying to untie the boats and steal them. Peter jumped out of the wagon with a tire iron and a barking dog who charged at them and scared them away. I slept, comfortable and safe, in the hotel.

The next morning we found a transmission-repair shop that would take us right away. Four hundred dollars later we were able to take off. But by now, of course, it was the late afternoon; once again, we arrived at Annapolis a day late. The hooting and cheering did not overcome the displeasure of the show management, who finally forgave us after hearing the story.

We'd missed the first show, we were late for the second show — and the third show? Late again. And once again, our peers took great delight in heckling us as we put up our stand while the show was running. And once again, the show staff was not impressed.

Getting reasonably priced hotels near the show was impossible, so many exhibitors found rooms in local houses. The residents turned over their houses for a big fat fee that could pay a year's mortgage; still, it was cheaper than the hotels. We could afford neither, so the first year we rented a motor home, thinking we could all live there and park near the show. That first night in the motor home was very cold, and we soon found out that there was no bedding or blankets. We slept in our clothes, and I managed to use the plastic shower curtain for a blanket. We had no idea how to operate the heater; thankfully, we figured it out before the next night.

The third year we had the brilliant idea of renting a houseboat. This turned out to be the party boat of the show. The crew and liveaboards included my mother and Rose, plus a host of friends and employees. Our first party aboard that boat quickly grew raucous. The next morning, bodies were just strewn around the boat. Mom took it all in stride. She seemed to be enjoying herself.

Things got worse the next night — again, thanks to a sailmaker. Only, this time it was our own North Sails Pewaukee man, Charlie Miller, caught "destroying city property." They were just paper bags over parking meters saying, "No Parking," but the notorious redneck police caught him and charged him and whisked him off to jail.

A half dozen of us and my mother went to the jail to bail him out. But the processing took a very long time, so we just sort of camped out most of the night on the jailhouse steps. Finally after paying the $200 bail money, Charlie was released. But he still had to appear the next day for a trial.

As he was walking down the hall looking for the courtroom in which he'd been ordered to appear, a man asked him if he could help. When Charlie told him where he was going, the man said that was a coincidence, since he was the judge who would try him. The judge asked Charlie what it was all about, then ordered in the court stenographer, the policeman who'd arrested him, and the lawyer assigned to represent him. The judge opened the case, recorded Charlie's statement, and dismissed it before anyone could say anything. He then apologized on behalf of the city and admonished the cop for being so aggressive and not just warning Charlie to stop.

A good ending to a good story.

1980 MOSCOW OLYMPIC SAILING VENUE

Andre Kislov was the vice chairman of the 1980 Moscow Olympic Games. Arvit Tetsman was the managing director of a large shipyard in Tallinn, the capital of Estonia. In 1979, Andre and Arvit had traveled to Pewaukee to negotiate an agreement with us to supply all of the hardware for the Olympic boats they were going to build. They also needed us to teach their people how to build strong and lightweight 470s to a very tight tolerance. One day during the negotiations, Andre and Arvit were sitting on a bench outside watching the construction of our new building on Wisconsin Avenue. They seemed to be mesmerized watching the masons building one of the walls with cinder blocks. One man was mixing the cement mud and applying it to the palette of the mason, who scraped off what he needed and applied it to the next block, carefully lining it up with a string to make sure everything was square. The mason then tapped it in place and scraped off the extra mud. The speed and accuracy with which the wall grew was a process unfamiliar to Andre and Arvit.

During our meetings, they said they felt we should be delighted with the honor of supplying them with boats and equipment for free. We explained that this was our business and that we were not subsidized by the government to do them such a favor. The negotiations were not going well. As a negotiation strategy, we said if they built the boats, we would teach them. They completely ignored our arguments and would repeat their request for us to supply everything free of charge, but sweeten it up with an Olympic trinket such as a medal, a flag, or a pin. In the evenings we'd go to dinner. One night Andre bragged how he could outdrink any American. To Peter this was a challenge, and they went glass-for-glass. Peter was still standing when the big Russian went down in his chair.

We didn't come to an agreement, and they eventually asked us to continue negotiations in Moscow. We did not like the idea, but Peter said he'd go. They screwed up in getting him a visa on time, so they shifted the meeting to Paris — an arrangement we were much more comfortable with anyway. Andre and a senior Russian diplomat in Paris were running the so-called "negotiations." This time the technique was bullying, and they wanted to start early each morning and go late into the evening. Peter told them he was a late sleeper; he said he would be available around noon and that he would have to leave around 5 p.m. to sightsee in Paris.

This drove them crazy. Finally they said they had had enough and were not going to do business with us. Peter had been armed with numbers that Mitch and I had worked out, showing the lowest we could go. In fact, we still had room. When the negotiations broke down, Peter said no thanks and walked out. The Russian diplomat chased him down and said Andre was a buffoon, that he didn't know anything about diplomacy, and that they'd be happy to accept our offer. It was important for them to save face, so we made sure they still got a good price. The only condition they had was to have us travel to and sign the agreement in Tallinn. We agreed.

Behind the Iron Curtain

Later that year Peter, Ruth, and I flew into Helsinki and took a Russian ship to Tallinn. Ruth took her camera out and started to take some pictures. A crewman motioned to her to stop immediately. He was very threatening. The only food on board was sliced eel, which was not something we Midwesterners could handle. When we arrived, we stood in a long line going through customs. A couple of young soldiers glared at us and tried to look threatening, but to no avail. Two big black cars arrived and some men pulled us out of the line and into the cars. Andre and Arvit were there, so it was nice to see some friendly faces.

The first thing on the agenda was lunch, which we were happy to hear. But you guessed it: the only thing offered was sliced eel. They wanted to drink vodka first, then sign the contract when we were half drunk from all of the toasts they came up with. We looked it over first, and it seemed to be accurate so we signed it. We also discovered that the eel was palatable with a shot of their very smooth, very cold vodka.

The next few days were spent sightseeing. While we weren't assigned a minder from the government, we were never left alone. Peter, Ruth, and I saw some beautiful churches that were shut down and converted into government facilities. There were limited numbers of newspapers printed and instead of printing more, people had to wait in long lines hoping to get one. Peter was interviewed in Tallinn by a news channel for an update on sailing in the Olympics. We then watched masons building one of the Olympic dormitories, and the difference was huge. Their blocks were so big it took two men to carry them. They would stick a pole through them and hoist them on their shoulders, heaving them up on top of the previous block. A huge amount of cement that had been applied first oozed out between the seams. That was it. The block was not lined up; the cement was not scraped off; holes and gaps were everywhere: it was just a big mess. When we questioned how they were going to finish it off, they said they would grind it smooth. We asked why the blocks were so big. The reason, they explained, was that the government-contracted factory was rewarded based on the total weight of the blocks, and of course big ones weighed more. The size was not their problem.

We went through the enormous government-owned boat factory. It looked to be about the size of a football field and was not quite finished. The factory that made the door handles was behind, and there were no alternatives. In addition, hundreds of ventilator fans were lying on the roof for months, because they arrived early and were not ready to be installed. There was a sail loft in the building. When we went through it, the workers were sleeping and didn't even bother to get up since they couldn't be fired.

The boats they were building for the Olympics had a similar level of quality. A few ladies would dip the fiberglass cloth into a pan of resin, then lay the soggy piece in the mold. They didn't even use gloves. The resin pooled in the bottom of the mold and usually began to harden before they had used it up. The boats weighed a ton, and the girls' hands were raw from the catalyzed resin. They needed help. What a system. Even three decades later, I wonder if they'll ever catch up.

Halloween with the Soviets

The agreement called for us to train a few of the Soviet workers in Pewaukee. It was a good idea but not what they expected. They sent three workers from Estonia: one woman and two men. In addition there was a Moscow woman organizing the purchasing of materials they needed, and one female KGB agent to make sure they wouldn't run away.

Halloween with our Soviet visitors, 1979

When I went to the airport to pick them up, the KGB agent noticed the Native American names like Pewaukee, Milwaukee, Oconomowoc, and Waukesha. She immediately started to say she heard how we treated them and that we put them in reservations, which were like prison camps. She asked if that was true, and I said most of them lived on reservations by choice, attended regular schools, owned their own houses, and were free to be on or off the reservation. She scoffed and gave me an "I told you so" look. I responded that "the difference was that we could talk freely about our country without fear. If we were in Russia, we wouldn't even be able to have this conversation." She was going to be a real pest, but we figured it would only take some time to soften her up and we might as well start right away.

It just so happened that they arrived on Halloween, and our people were dressed beautifully. They had every costume you could imagine: pregnant nuns, monsters, aliens, bucket heads, old geezers, cross-dressers, and a host of very creative costumes the ladies in our canvas department had made up. After my little discussion with the KGB, I decided I wasn't going to say anything about it. I led them in as though this were normal, and they were totally confused and didn't know whether to laugh, believe this was normal, or feel insulted because there was no such thing as Halloween in Russia.

It was the beginning of a wonderful chance to let them see what freedom was all about. For the next few weeks they went to our peoples' houses for dinner, drove the company cars, went shopping on their own, and were left unsupervised in a big mall near Chicago for several hours. They all came out with very large plastic bags that were all the same. We thought they were probably jeans, but to our surprise they sheepishly showed us what was in the bags. It was Kotex. Personal hygiene in the USSR was not a priority. When they were getting ready to leave, there were lots of tearful goodbyes between true friends. Even Miss Hardnose KGB was crying after we handed her an NFL football with fake Packer signatures (that we put on), and had come to a completely different attitude about our way of life. It was a great experience and a lot of fun.

Fending Off the FBI

Two weeks after they left, the FBI arrived and wanted to know where the Russians were. When we said they'd left two weeks earlier, they got really snotty and asked if we had watched them the whole time. We said we thought that was the FBI's job. We then asked if they ever talked to the State Department, because the information was all in the visas issued. It didn't give us a lot of confidence in our intelligence system.

Meanwhile, the Russians owed us $50,000, due upon delivery. But then President Carter pulled the plug on the American team going to the 1980 Olympics in Moscow, and we thought we might not see our money. That was a huge amount of money for our small company. Peter traveled to DC and talked to the people in the Russian division of the State Department. He asked if they thought we'd be able to get it. They assured us that despite the political scene, business was going on as usual, and if we had given them good product for their money, we should eventually get paid.

Weeks passed, and the Russians finally answered our faxes and said a check had been cut for us and should be there by now. Nothing happened and finally they said another check had been issued and sent through the Chemical Bank of New York. The bank kept insisting that they had not received anything. They were lying, and there were two checks at the Chemical Bank for $50,000 each that they were holding to earn interest. Some banks held off payments in order to increase their investments. We were furious and apologized to the Russians and returned one of the checks.

THE ITALIAN CONNECTION (1985)

At the Genoa International Boat Show in 1985, I was approached by a young man inquiring about our interest in buying or selling a winch-manufacturing company. The company name was Barbarossa (Italian for "Red Beard"), and the man was Luca Bassani, the son of one of the wealthiest men in Italy. His father was the creator of the Bassani Ticino Company, which made electrical components for homes, offices, and the auto industry. The main plant was in Varese near Lake Como and employed over 4,000 people. They also had plants in France and Brazil.

Luca and his brother Tony were avid sailors and very good. They'd won the European Six Meter Championships several times. Their father wanted them to learn about running a company, so he bought Barbarossa for them to run and make a profit. The company was well staffed, and the winches were beautifully designed and manufactured. But quality control, service, on-time deliveries, marketing, and communication needed more attention. Since these were Harken's strong points and we needed a winch line, we all felt it would be a good fit.

We agreed to continue our discussions and made plans for our patent attorney and friend Russ Pyle to travel to Italy with us. Our group was Peter, Russ, Art, and I. Peter and I have a rule about flying on separate planes in case one goes down. When we arrived, we rented a big and very powerful Fiat Lancia. Because high speeds were much more common there and were overlooked by most of the police, we put the pedal to the metal and screamed along the autostrade at upwards of 120 mph. Everyone wanted to drive, so we took turns and tried to match or exceed the other guy. This was the team that flew on separate planes in case of an accident. Go figure.

Signor Tartaruga

Barbarossa was located in the town of Lomazzo, halfway between Milan and Como. It was housed in an adjacent building on the same property. There was a small garden in the back with a strawberry patch where Signor Tartaruga lived. He was a large snapping turtle that would wander into the machine shop each day to visit everyone, then return to his garden after an hour or so. He definitely had the run of the place.

One of the reasons we liked the deal was the location. The business was near the foothills of the Alps by Lago di Como, a huge deep-water lake stretching over thirty kilometers in a north-south direction. The city of Como was on the lake's south end. Cernobbio was a city adjacent to Como and was where we usually stayed. We leased an apartment there a few years later. It was a magnificent sight next to the Lake, with a piazza in front and hotels, restaurants, and shops all around. The thought of staying there was an enticement and helped our decision to make the deal. These days George Clooney has a villa there, and Madonna frequently stays in the area. Villa de Este, one of world's great five-star hotels, was next door.

The people at the company were very special. We had been told that we were crazy to consider buying an Italian company since the cultures were too different. Obviously they had never worked with Raffaele Vernocchi and Luciano Bonassi, the sales manager and chief engineer respectively.

Luciano Bonassi

Raffaele Vernocchi

Neither spoke English, but it did not seem to matter. Raffael was always excited and funny, and he used his hands very clearly so we could understand him. Luciano and Peter bonded and took friendly jabs at each other. He was an amazing engineer who started each design with pen and ink, including complex gear trains. All of the other engineers worked on computers but could not produce finished drawings at the speed of Bonassi's pen. They both died of cancer in their sixties. We miss them.

We reached an agreement with Luca. We traded him some of our shares for his company and bought the rest with cash. Luca would get a seat on our board, which we were happy with. He was smart and financially strong — not one of our strengths. In addition, the engineering manager at Bassani Ticino, Federico Giua, wanted to work for the company. So we got a top manager in the deal who had managed 400 engineers at BT. We were off and running in the winch business.

Federico had a different style of running a company than Peter and I had. As the years passed, this proved to be difficult for all of us. Eventually, we decided to part ways. This was all done without any animosity, and we remain friends.

We now needed a manager, and we spent months interviewing candidates with no success. Peter and I decided to look inside Barbarossa and were impressed with the energy, sailing knowledge, and English of one of our staff. He was only 26 years old, had no university education, and was very inexperienced. That did not appear to be the credentials an employer would consider, but we had a good feeling and decided to check with Vernocchi and Bonassi. They both said it was okay with them as long as he didn't screw up!

Giampaolo Spera was our candidate. Of course, he was surprised at our interest in having him be our assistant manager, with Peter as the manager until we felt he could manage alone. He'd never be really alone, though, since Peter, Art Mitchel, Bob Sweet, and I were there frequently to back him up.

Giampi proved to be the right kind of man we were looking for. He was a quick learner in almost everything and a voracious reader of business books. He was good with his people and customers and a superb sailor. Under his guidance Harken Italy is in a brand–new, 86,000-square-foot factory with 80 employees and is a profitable operation.

THE WATERBUG (1985)

Gary Hoyt has always had a passion for boating innovations and we have great respect for his creative mind. He got us involved in a number of his ideas including the Waterbug and the Mallard (one- and two-seat pedal boats), and various winglike structures. There is about a one in ten chance of a new idea getting to market. The Waterbug was one of them.

It was winter and the lakes in Wisconsin were frozen when we finished the first prototype, so we needed to find an indoor pool to perform the test. The manager of the Country Springs Hotel agreed to let us use their pool if it could be done in a few hours and before the pool opened for the guests.

We called Gary in Newport and told him we had a big problem. We had put it in the pool before all the ballast was loaded and it had rolled over and sunk. The manager was furious and not being very understanding. We were going to have a hell of a time getting it out with it sitting on the bottom of the pool. Gary was quite upset at first and blamed it on us for not putting enough ballast in. We decided it was time to tell him it was a prank — that we had really pulled his chain and told him that he was too serious.

Being able to handle large waves, Waterbugs were fun to cruise in on both the ocean and the inland lakes

Actually the Waterbug tested perfectly and was a delight to pedal in all conditions including big waves. Sitting in a padded seat in the recumbent position she could cruise at about four knots and was unsinkable. It was cute looking, comfortable, fun, and it was safe since it had 300 pounds of ballast and could not turn over. The unique pedal drive system used a chain in a Mobius loop and worked very well. It had one problem. It cost too much, which affected sales.

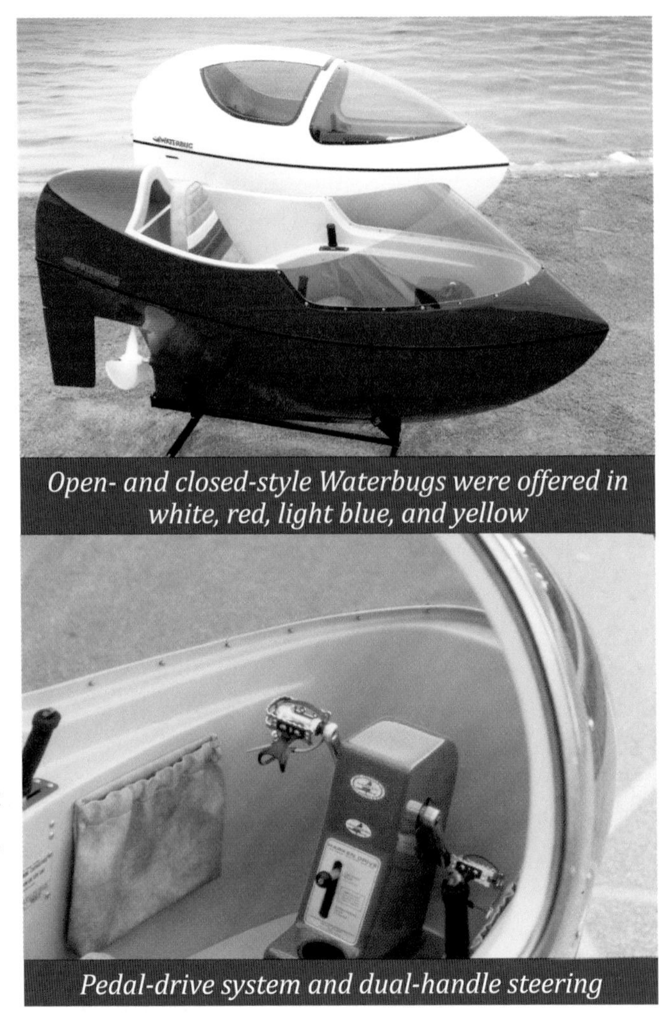

Open- and closed-style Waterbugs were offered in white, red, light blue, and yellow

Pedal-drive system and dual-handle steering

MILLER TIME IN MOSCOW (1991)

The following story takes place in Moscow, Tampa, and Milwaukee in the early 1990s. The common thread was that all of the players were sailors. I was only involved in a small way but had a great vantage point since Peter was a major figure in this unique tale. Each one of us had a role but we were drawn together by the adventure of being close to the massive changes that were happening in the Soviet Union.

Mikhail Gorbachev had just stepped down and Boris Yeltsin was in. Capitalism had been introduced and was out of control, but once tasted, was unstoppable. We ended up being right in the middle of this when we founded a little beer-distribution company, First Republic, the exclusive importer and distributor of Miller Beer for Moscow and Odessa. The company was a real player in the process since it introduced the major principles of marketing, quality control, inventory, on-time delivery, and competition to a country that had no clue about running a business. Rick Grajirena, a champion sailor, sailmaker, and entrepreneur from Tampa, Florida, founded the company with Peter after encountering the opportunity by chance during a trip to Russia.

Rick had asked Peter to go to Russia with him to explore the opportunities of having some parts made. Russia had an enormous pool of educated engineers, machinists, skilled workers, machinery, raw materials, and buildings to produce military equipment. Many of these people were without work since Gorbachev gave up trying to win the arms race. Reagan had pushed him to the wall, and it had worked.

Rick grew up sailing in St. Petersburg, Florida. In grammar school he was a terrible student. But then, luckily for him, he was invited to go sailing, a pursuit that became his passion, his sport, and his business later in life. He became a champion sailor in many classes, from high-performance dinghies to big ocean racers. He worked as a sailmaker with North Sails and also had his own sail loft. He made fast sails and was in great demand to go racing aboard the yachts of his customers.

We met Rick at a regatta for 470 Olympic-class sailboats. Rick had purchased his boat from us and used North Sails. His wife, Mary, worked for North Sails under Olympic champion Peter Barrett, our former partner in Scanda and now the North Sails executive vice president. They worked out of a large container in our parking lot, so we were all pretty close.

In 1990 Rick got involved with the Russian entry in the Whitbread Round the World Race, which was going to start in Ft. Lauderdale. This was one of the most difficult races in the world, and the event drew tens of thousands of spectators in many countries where the boats stopped. Among the contenders was a Russian entry — very unusual, since the Russians had never participated in sailing events except the Olympics and other world-champion events in small boats.

The boat, named *Fasizi*, was from Odessa, the Ukrainian seaport on the Black Sea. The project, called Odessa 200, received some of the funding from the city, but not enough to support this very expensive race. The boat and crew, on a shoestring budget, hoped to raise money at each stop from donations by people who took some pity on this underdog. They were very popular and were invited to many cocktail parties by the wealthy people who were curious to see real live Russians from the "Evil Empire." Another source of income was the sale of their very popular T-shirts with "The Russians are Coming" emblazoned on their backs and *Fasizi* and Odessa 200 on the front.

The fleet of boats was in Ft. Lauderdale getting fitted out and prepared for the race. *Fasizi* was badly in need of sails, and some of the crew went to visit Rick, whom they knew from international sailing events, at his Tampa sail loft to see if they could get a deal. They renewed old friendships and kept the boat in Tampa for fundraising. Rick was very helpful in introducing them to the wealthy sailors in Tampa and St. Petersburg. The very popular leader of the team, Kuli, ended up staying at Rick's home for seven months.

Back to Beer

Rick had developed extensive experience in Russia and even ran seminars on how to do business in Russia. In one such project he worked with dentists who were interested in upgrading the deplorable dental system in Russia. Rick really wanted to become a successful businessman instead of a professional sailor and sailmaker. Russia was an opportunity, and he had an edge.

One of his plans was to help companies make things using the materials and manufacturing available. He got Peter interested, and the two of them visited a number of factories and engineers anxious to do business. As it turned out, the quality and reliability of the titanium parts were totally unacceptable. They then visited Ulyanovsk, a city near the Ural Mountains, where there were military factories formerly off limits but now looking for business.

From there they went to Odessa for more meetings and to visit the home of Odessa 200. The passengers on their plane cheered and clapped when it landed safely on Odessa's potholed runway. The man sitting next to them reached into his briefcase and pulled out a can of Old Milwaukee Beer, rewarding himself for surviving another trip. Later they were riding an elevator in their hotel when a man asked them if they knew how he could buy two containers of Old Milwaukee. This was an average brand of beer in the United States, but in the former Soviet Union they felt it was a luxury compared to their beer.

These two events sparked an idea. Instead of exporting Russian products to the United States, how about importing U.S. products to Russia? Peter knew a vice president of Miller Brewing Company who was a sailor. He and Rick did a preliminary market analysis and made an appointment to see him. The Miller executive was interested; he told them to complete a plan. He'd get them an appointment with the top man at Miller International in London.

Using Russian marketing students to cover all of Moscow, First Republic had a highly accurate analysis, checking every grocery store, hotel, restaurant, and kiosk, section by section, in Moscow. It was a first in market analysis for the Russian market, and it really impressed the Miller people. Miller and Heineken both gave the fledlging company a chance and appointed it as the exclusive distributor for Moscow.

The agreement had some difficult conditions, however, such as no credit at all. Still, all that was needed was money, and it was surprisingly easy to get investors who wanted to get in on this unique venture. Many of the investors were from Pewaukee, including me. I put in $20,000, as did many of our fellow sailors. Peter was the major investor and spent significant time in Moscow helping out.

The demand for a really good beer instead of the Russian dishwater was fantastic. Beer in bottles became a status symbol. Their primary customers were the Western-style hotels and upscale restaurants. With some good old American marketing, the beer became available in the grocery stores and bars. They formed the "Cold Patrol," a group of beautiful women in black and gold outfits. The Cold Patrol would be at stores and bars that took on Miller Beer. They had advertising painted on their delivery trucks — a rare sight, since most Russian businesses were afraid of hijackers if it was known what was in the trucks. On the contrary, advertising limitations was old school, which had to change.

At Moscow's Sheremetyevo airport, First Republic placed a huge, dramatic Miller Beer ad in the main terminal showing a massive Miller truck charging into the terminal. First Republic held Super Bowl parties, New Year's parties, and World Series parties for American expatriates. The

The eight-foot, back-lit sign at Moscow's Sheremetyevo airport

events were extremely popular, and the participating hotels stocked up dozens of cases of Miller Beer. There was no end to the list of customers. All that was needed was plenty of beer, especially during holidays and events.

They built and trained a staff — a manager, a bookkeeper, delivery-truck drivers, and a young American salesman who lived over there and spoke Russian — to run the operation. The salesman liked the girls, and there were plenty.

Although Rick, Peter, and another American partner spent time over there, they didn't spend enough. The Russians had terrible work habits and didn't mind taking advantage of the trust which they'd been given. There were numerous problems with the manager and some of the staff.

Peter wearing his obtained Russian military outfit upon his return

Soon it became clear that running the operation from Florida wasn't going to work. But Rick didn't want to move his family to Russia and Peter was running our company. They hired a young American man in the United States who ran it for a while, but the problems were more than a long-distance manager could solve.

Containers Full of Beer — And No One to Move Them

It was important to have lots of beer available for New Year's, the peak of demand. Rick had ordered seven containers to handle the order. It was shipped sometime in September or October to the Baltic port of Riga. From Riga the containers were scheduled to be trucked to Moscow on a convoy of seven trucks. This was organized by Yellow Freight.

The ships arrived on schedule, only to find out the truck drivers had found a more lucrative load and just took off. Peter called Yellow Freight, and they tried to pass the buck. Miller wouldn't help, and the beer stayed on the docks for month after month. It took almost four months to finally pick up the containers. To make things worse, the beer had frozen, which spoiled it. When they eventually looked inside the containers, they found some good beer still unfrozen in the center of the load, but it was too little too late. To top it off, Miller demanded their money and would not even give First Republic terms to pay over a longer period.

The Case of the Trapped Beer

The New Year's shipment was a big blow to First Republic, and it wasn't their last hurdle. Spring that year came in with a lot of rain. Several containers of First Republic beer were stored in a warehouse in Moscow. The warehouse was in the basement with a ramp leading down to the overhead door so that a truck could go down to be loaded. But with the constant rain coming down, a massive mudslide had closed off the entrance. It was a mess, and to clear the entrance they would need a backhoe. Peter and Rick were scratching their heads about what to do.

Then, an idea struck them. While trucks couldn't pass, people could still get in and out of the warehouse through a smaller door. They found a few dozen Russian soldiers standing around nearby, so they went over and negotiated a deal. If the soldiers would unload the beer into the truck, they could have all the beer they could drink. The soldiers jumped at the opportunity and formed a big line to pass the cartons to the truck. Rick was able to find another warehouse, and once again a little Yankee ingenuity won the day.

Other impediments included taxes that changed on a daily basis from almost nothing to 200 percent, as well as problems getting our overseas staff to work hard and deal honestly. Miller had not given us decent payment terms nor advertising support, which compounded the problem. The mixture of the Russian business climate, regulations, dishonest managers, politics, lawyers, as well as Miller Beer's constant demand for money put massive strains on the operation. Seventy plus years of a society that did not reward those who worked hard had serious effects. We never had a problem with the Russian Mafia though — for some reason they left us completely alone. Still, things did not improve.

Governor Tommy Thompson

Fritz Ruf was a good friend, advisor, and confidant, and he knew the ins and outs of the U.S. government. He helped us on numerous occasions and had been part of the Tommy Thompson administration. Thompson was Wisconsin's longest-serving governor, from 1987 to 2001, then was U.S. Secretary of Health and Human Services from 2001 to 2005 in the George W. Bush administration.

In 1993, the governor was to lead a trade mission to Russia and wanted to see some of Moscow before he got into the more formal part of his visit. Fritz suggested that Peter and I could meet him and be his guide during his stay. We'd met him before, and he liked the idea.

We met the governor and his small entourage, including Fritz, in the VIP section of the airport, and were whisked through immigration and customs. We had rented two Volkswagen buses and packed everyone and the luggage in, including a bodyguard, which the embassy insisted upon. Wouldn't you know it? His name was Igor, and he was a professional wrestler.

The flight to Moscow is very long; when you get to Europe, you're still only halfway there. Our group was really tired except for the governor. It was quite late so we suggested a nightclub with Russian comedians and lots of beautiful girls dancing like the Radio City Rockettes. Tommy was wide awake the whole time, while the rest of us slept in our seats.

The following days and nights were packed, and Thompson had no end to his energy level. We toured a cemetery for important people where each grave had a uniquely designed marker relevant to the person's life instead of a typical headstone. One famous heart surgeon had a red crystal heart about the size of a football on a pedestal over his grave. The cosmonauts who'd died were in a common grave that had a 4-by-8-foot stainless-steel plaque with their names and pictures marking the spot. Yuri Gagarin was on the plaque.

Khrushchev's grave had been relocated to a remote spot, since he was not in favor at the time.

We visited the famous Moscow McDonald's, and it was amazing. There was a line of Muscovites about a hundred yards long and four abreast waiting for their turn. The line moved at a rapid pace, and after a few minutes we were in. About 20 stations took orders, and our burgers were ready in no time. Most of the locals bought a lot of extra burgers to feed the family. The décor was interesting: six-foot-high, clear-plastic models of most of the famous buildings in the world — the Eiffel Tower, the Leaning Tower of Pisa, the Empire State Building — decorated the place.

We went to see one of the cathedrals, which happened to be having a service at the time. We stood in a small crowd at the back since the pews were packed. We got reprimanded by an old lady for whispering something amongst ourselves — She was really mad, but it was pretty funny to us at the time.

We had dinner one night at Tren Mos, which was very similar to the restaurant in Casablanca frequented by the ex-pats. The name was a combination of Tren (for Trenton, New Jersey) and Moscow. Flags from the different states surrounded the restaurant, and Tommy presented them with the Wisconsin state flag.

At night we usually went to a casino; it was good fun. One night Tommy was being honored at the American embassy, and the room was filled with dignitaries, including some

Tommy Thompson and Olaf, 1993

Russian cosmonauts. He gave a speech and included First Republic, which was very nice. We took lots of pictures at the Kremlin, Lenin's Tomb, Red Square, St. Basil's Cathedral with the beautiful onion domes, and one with us and the Governor in front of a large Miller Beer Truck with the cathedral in the background.

That's all from the great beer caper in Moscow. All I can say is it was the best $20,000 I ever spent.

GOOD FRIENDS, GOOD BUSINESS, GOOD FUN AROUND THE WORLD

Jib Furling systems are one of the most important products that we sell. They are designed in our engineering department and produced primarily by Frentzel Products Inc. in their Milwaukee plant. We have been working with Tom Frentzel for well over 30 years. His son Tom Frentzel Jr. now runs the business for him.

Tom and I assembled one of the first units in St. Thomas for a sailor who is a well-known journalist, Don Street, who swore he would never use a Harken furler on his boat. We challenged him to try one out on his famous 44-foot boat *Iolaire*. After a week of sailing with it, he was so impressed that he wrote a glowing report on the system.

One time, we traded a furling system for a week of cruising on a 65-foot boat, *Sargasso,* together with both of our families. The weather and winds didn't cooperate, but it was not a bad deal.

Every year in November all of our distributors from around the world meet at METS (Marine Equipment Trade Show), in Amsterdam. It is the largest and most important show in the world for equipment used on boats.

We have a large display that is unique in that it is an international booth supported by us and the distributors. Here we show off our newest items to the boatbuilders, naval architects, retailers, other distributors, and anyone who is a customer or potential customer. Our equipment range is from boats like the 7-foot Optimist class to 250-foot megayachts, so we can meet a wide variety of customers at the show. Several offices in our stand are always full of customers wanting specifications, prices, market trends, and the occasional complainers. It is a very busy time, one that calls for a little relaxing at the hotel bar, followed by dinner and wine.

Most of our distributors have been with us for over 30 years, and we've been together so many times that strong friendships have developed. It is one of the real assets of this business. We share our love for the sport of sailing, but that's not the only thing that binds us. We frequently stay at each other's houses and socialize with the wives and the kids.

Patrick Rieupeyrout has been our French distributor for over 30 years and has an extensive knowledge of our hardware. We usually stay at each other's houses when visiting. When my two older kids were in first and second grade, they took French at their elementary school. When their teacher heard we had a man from France visiting, she asked if he could come for show-and-tell. The kids were very excited and one of the children asked what a Frenchman looks like. Patrick kind of pointed to himself awkwardly and tried to help them put the puzzle pieces together. We had a good laugh about it afterwards.

I already mentioned Jukka Herrala, our very successful Finnish distributor, who is always laughing and joking. We always have a good time with Jukka.

The friendship between Peter and Göran Rutergson, forged back at the Avalon Hotel in Miami in 1976, was instrumental in getting our equipment on the Swedish America's Cup boat, which at the time was the only Cup contender that was willing to try out our new concepts of a high-load ball and a roller-bearing block. It started our complete dominance of the AC boats today.

Peter Frisch and Eddy Eich are our German distributors. With Germany being a big market for us, I was apprehensive about choosing them and asked Peter and Mitch to give me their opinion. After meeting the two, without hesitation Peter and Mitch said, "Sign them up." Since then, Peter and Eddy have consistently been one our best and biggest distributors. We sometimes argue, but good friends can do that without rancor.

Robbert Verboon from Holland is a very smart engineer and naval architect. He is full of energy, gets things done, and even takes us on canal trips in his open wooden boat when we visit. Robbert's wife, Luuke, is a stitch and always good for a laugh. Robbert took over the business when the founder and our friend, Fred Imhoff, retired.

Then there is Luis Martino, our Spanish distributor, who looks like and acts like Inspector Clouseau from the Pink Panther movies. Around 1990 we had organized a huge weeklong work-and-play session on the island of Sint Maarten for many of our managers and our best customers. Our Caribbean distributor, Robbie Ferron, organized six Lasers for the event for any of us to use. Luis took one and soon sailed right onto a reef. Without shoes on, he dragged the boat across the entire reef instead of turning around. When at a toll-road pay station during a later visit to Barcelona, he drove in, then went and got out his purse from the back seat, opened it, found the money, paid the toll, closed the purse, and returned it to the back seat. By this time a long line of cars had formed blowing their horns. It did not even faze Luis; we love him and kid him.

Tad Ikami from Japan is absolutely certain that there was no attack on Pearl Harbor and that the atom bomb is a myth. He says my father was a "guest" of the Japanese during his internment in a Japanese concentration camp. In spite of his beliefs, he can really sell blocks. He races a Dragon, is an international judge, and has been with us for four decades. Tad knows I do not like sushi or fishy stuff, so he always leads me to a restaurant where I cannot read the menu and tells me it is a noodle-specialty place, which is okay to me. He does not tell me that every creature in the ocean is under the noodles. When he comes to Wisconsin, I make sure to give him a big slab of fatty roast beef, which he hates.

Remembering Marty Rieck — and Art Schmickter

Art Schmickter was a fictitious customer that Marty, our global sales manager, came up with to give our poor new tech service guy, Mike Lee, something to deal with for his first day at work and for many months thereafter over 30 plus emails. Marty was highly respected for his knowledge and ability to lead with a little humor thrown in. He was also a great practical joker, and this little caper says it all. Here are Mike Lee's words about his relationship with Art Schmickter.

"I happened to meet Art Schmickter via email on my first day of work in Tech Service. Art was having all kinds of problems with his Harken furler, and every suggestion I made to him to help solve his problems usually led him and his old buddy Jake into some crazy adventure. One time they needed to get the forestay back into the furling foils, but they couldn't figure out how to do it, so they sat down and finished off a bottle of brandy until an easy solution came to them. They simply stood the foils up on end next to Art's barn, went to the top of the roof, and dropped a tracer line down. Another adventure even left them stranded on the flooded Raccoon River, where Old Man Packet had to rescue them with his Case tractor.

For months emails went back and forth with Art and me. One problem always led to another. Why didn't I just pick up the phone and call him? Well, Art had a stoma in his throat as a result of years of smoking and wasn't able to speak. The whole thing seemed a little suspicious, but there wasn't much I could do about it as a new employee. I kept pushing on with Art, my difficult customer, day in and day out.

At one point in the summer Art was so appreciative of all my help, he was going to hook up the Luger to his car and come and visit me at Harken.

"For your thoughtfulness I would like to bring you a hog," he wrote. "Do you have a freezer? My neighbor Ralf raises some of the nicest-looking Iowa hogs you have ever seen, and he'll butcher one for me the day before I leave. If you get a freezer cleared out, I can fill it up again. I usually fill the trunk of my Maverick so that will give you an idea of the volume of space you will need. Everybody always enjoys a good rasher of bacon in the morning and you should have enough for a few months of fine eating."

Eventually I figured out how to do a reverse email search to see where they were coming from. Art's messages weren't coming from Iowa City but from Port Washington, Wisconsin. That could only mean one person was behind the email, Marty Rieck. Marty was famous for pranks throughout the company, and this one was one of the biggest and best. Sadly I never had a chance to reciprocate, as Marty passed away on his boat just days after I was on to him. Marty was one of those who made Harken a fun place to work."

Marty Rieck and his wife, Susie, 1995

Marty and his wife, Susie, were sailing on their trimaran *Blue Moose* by Hessel Bay in Michigan, when he suffered a massive heart attack and passed away before help could arrive. Our customers and people here all loved him, and his loss was felt by all who came in contact with him.

Over the last four decades, we've been lucky to attract lots of people who make it a fun place to work.

Chapter Eight

The Need for Speed: Sailing at Technology's Edge (1980–Present)

IF WE PAY, WE PLAY

Over all the early years of our business, our decision-making process often started at a bar as we tipped a few and discussed whether we should or should not invest in a particular project, process, or product. Often enough, we went ahead with the more outlandish projects. Today the company is more formal and less fun, but it's probably for the best. However, we do need to exercise our independence once in a while. We've been known to go ahead on a project without putting it through an expensive review and years-long, government-style study. Our style has resulted in many adventures and has been very successful over the years.

Sort of...

Peter's executive decision

Peter and I have one common philosophy regarding future major investments: if we pay, we play. This has proved to be fun and a great excuse to limit the myriad of requests we receive from folks who'd like us to pay for their fun. We've sponsored several large-scale events over the years, and they all seemed to center around speed. We do not like to go slow. Our Vanguard high-performance dinghies were all designed to go as fast as we could make them and be legal. Our favorite, if not our most frustrating sport, is iceboating: a combination of race-car driving and sailing. In the summer, I have *Stealth*, a 38-foot A-Scow, which has, by some standards of measurement, been referred to as the fastest standard-production monohull sailboat in the world.

In addition, we've engaged in several high-profile projects centered on speed. We attempted but failed to break the world's sailing speed record in a boat called *Slingshot*, and we developed and led a project to build *Procyon*, a 65-foot cruising boat that was as fast as an all-out racer. I crossed the Atlantic Ocean in one of the fastest boats in the world, the giant 110-foot catamaran *Team Adventure*.

Each has its own story.

SLINGSHOT AND THE WORLD SPEED SAILING RECORD (1980)

In 1980 Peter and I, together with North Sails and the Gougeon Brothers, created a small syndicate to break the world speed record — which at the time was held by *Crossbow* at 31.8 knots. (In 2012 Peter Larsen set the outright record at just over 68 knots.) We agreed to be part of this attempt and pay our share of the expenses, but only if we got to ride in the boat used for the event. One of the neat things about *Slingshot* was that she was designed to hold six people in the pod, which had been redesigned to be more like a seaplane hull that skipped on the water. So each company could put two people of their choice on board.

The story of *Slingshot* goes back to the early days of 1978 when a man by the name of Carl Thomas conceived the idea while he was adrift in the Atlantic Ocean in a life raft. One of his other adventures had gone awry, so he took the time before being rescued to dream up *Slingshot*.

The idea was to build a 60-foot-long proa with a large outrigger that extended outboard 44 feet and had a pod out at the end of the outrigger. From there, the helmsman steered while crew operated the sails and the outrigger, which could be cranked from one side to the other for leverage, forming a trimaran. The theory behind the rig was that it operated similar to a windsurfer, where the mast would lean over as far as 30 degrees and provide lift to the whole boat. This also allowed a larger sail to counterbalance the pressure of the wind on the sail. The challenge, however, was to keep the rig from falling over: when the outrigger was fully extended, there was no leeward shroud to keep the rig from falling. It was completely up to wind pressure to hold it and the outrigger needed to be recentered before slowing down to stop the boat.

Carl commissioned the Gougeon Brothers to build the boat in 1978, and he took it over to Weymouth, England, where the world speed trials were normally held. The wind, however, did not cooperate, and Carl was not able to achieve the record. He made another attempt the following year, but the boat had a breakdown that couldn't be repaired before the trials ended.

Terry Kohler, the owner of North Sails, talked with Peter Harken and Jan Gougeon about refitting the boat and chartering it for another attempt at the world record. It took Peter a couple of seconds to think it over, and we were in the game. The Gougeons also enthusiastically agreed to give it a try.

Mike Zuteck, Olaf Harken, Peter Harken, Jan Gougeon, Dan Reichelsdorfer, Ron Sherry, and John Maudlin on Slingshot

We had a lot of preparation to do. The first item on our list was to find a suitable location: flat water and high winds. We also needed to find an official to measure her speed runs and witness any attempt. I asked Bob Shields, the head measurer of the United States Yacht Racing Union, if he would accept the job; I knew he'd be fair and thorough. Bob agreed, and we chose a spot behind the breakwater at Galveston, Texas, in March and April when the winds were strong. There was a North Sails loft there and all the help we needed. The winds were also pretty steady and in the right direction. *Slingshot* was designed to operate at her best in 20 to 25 knots; *Crossbow*, by contrast, needed as much as 30 to 40 knots to compete.

The people of Galveston had really gotten to know about the event that was happening off their shores. Their hospitality was incredible, and many spectators came to watch. With our bright red *Slingshot* T-shirts identifying us, we were constantly being treated like celebrities. This made the whole event a lot more fun and something we will never forget.

Representing North Sails was Ron Sherry, a really hot iceboat sailor, and John Maudlin, who'd built his own boat to try for the world speed record. Dan Reichelsdorfer of North managed the logistics and support boat.

Making our way out to the pod after tacking

Jan Gougeon, founder of the famous WEST System brand of epoxy resin, was our driver. He was also an international DN iceboat champion. *Slingshot* had hydraulic steering and a hose that ran to the end of the rack so the helmsman could steer from the windward side. Also on the Gougeon team was Mike Zutech, nicknamed Z-Square, since he looked at every problem mathematically. Mike, a NASA physicist, invented a system we called the Zutalator: he connected lines to each one of the battens so that he could adjust the camber of the sails and keep lots of wind pressure on the sail when the boat was slowing down. The rig needed all the assistance it could get to keep the mast up.

Peter's job was to handle the jib, which he did from the front of the pod. My job was to winch the rack in or out from the main hull. After I'd extended it to its full 44 feet, I'd run up the crossbeam and jump into my seat. At one point in our speed trials, we did record a speed of 38 knots.

The beauty of *Slingshot* was her reliability. Many other boats built specially for record breaking had inherent problems that kept them in the repair shop most of the time. We frequently made as many as 10 runs a day with no breakdowns. However, we did have a few — the most exciting of which was when Jan lost his steering.

Taking it easy on Slingshot *between speed trials*

We were in about 18 knots of wind going at a speed of a little over 27 knots when we heard a muffled noise from the back of the boat. Through all the wind noise, this sound was a little hard to distinguish. But it got a little louder as the situation developed; before long, we heard Jan say, "I haven't got any steering." The boat peeled off and accelerated to a speed that probably equaled the world speed record. As the boat kept flying downwind, all eyes looked up: with the rack all the way out, the mast was going to come down. Peter, sitting in the front of the pod, figured it was coming down right on top of him, so he bailed out of the boat at around 30 knots and skipped across the water like a flat stone. I don't think he realized what it'd be like to hit the water at that speed.

Sure enough, the mast did come down — but slowly, and fortunately with very little damage. Still, the rudder needed repair, which took some time. The boat was out of commission for several days and the delays caused by the rudder and poor wind conditions decreased the chance of winds being strong enough to break the record.

In the meantime Peter and I traveled back and forth between Milwaukee and Houston to keep up with our day jobs. The rudder had been fixed, but while we were away, a small crew took *Slingshot* out for sea trials in very light air. She was under tow by the North support boat when all of a sudden the wind came

Slingshot — *the broken mast*

up to over 50 knots and the waves picked up to five feet. The boat was getting slammed around until the tow line finally broke. *Slingshot* took off with only two people on board, shooting downwind and aiming right at the breakwater. The crew tried to steer with the mast, but she smashed into the breakwater at full speed, and the hull broke into pieces in no time at all. The two crewmembers were able to scramble up the crossbeam and get off the boat before it was completely destroyed.

And that was the end of *Slingshot* — an expensive effort but really a lot of fun. A major disappointment was that we felt that the boat really did have the potential to break the record because of her reliability and the great design of having the sail lift the hull to decrease the drag.

ICEBOATING

Winter brings a new dimension to the area. Wisconsin is known for cold winters with blasts of air coming down from Canada. Temperatures usually hover just below freezing, but it will fluctuate between nose-hair-freezing sub-zero, or you will see Wisconsinites sunbathing in balmy 40-degree weather. Downhill and cross-country skiing are prevalent in the area, and if the lakes are smooth you'll see hockey rinks on the ice.

Peter's E Skeeter — Millennium Factor

Pewaukee Lake usually freezes over on the shallow end around the first of December. Two weeks later the deep end freezes, which gives us two opportunities to iceboat. The different freezing times of the surrounding lakes give more chances, since ice thickness and snow cover are critical factors to having ideal conditions for the sport. We kid about the fact that the ratio of time on the ice and time in the shop is easily about 500-to-1. But it is a labor of love.

I don't think that there is a sailing sport that we are identified with as much as iceboating. People are always asking us about the sport: when and where we do it, and how fast we go. Our pat answer is: Do you want to know the bar-talk speed, or the real speed?

Honestly, we don't know how fast we go; we're too busy racing to measure and taking advantage of any ice time we can get. Although nowadays, the more tech-savvy guys measure it with GPS and their phones. Our estimated speed of the unlimited Class A, E Skeeter is substantially over 100 mph, and on the other end of the scale is the International DN, which can go over 60 mph under good ice conditions. Between these are the Nites, Arrows, Renegades, and a myriad of small beginner boats. These are all front-steerers, meaning that the front runner, or skate, is connected to the steering mechanism using pedals, a tiller, or a steering wheel to turn the boat.

Class A, E Skeeter at full tilt

Around the turn of the twentieth century, iceboats were quite popular on frozen lakes and rivers in the East and Midwest. These boats were called stern-steerers for their single rear runner that acted like a rudder. There are still many iceboats in the region that were built in the 1930s; most have been restored with painstaking care. One of these, the *Deuce* — 56 feet long, her mast 52 feet high — is the largest active iceboat in the world. It takes a few hours to set her up, using a special trailer with a crane.

Every year there is a major regatta called the Northwest where stern-steerers congregate with many other classes and usually have two races per day for three days. It is spectacular to see them lined up on the starting line, their crews pushing like the devil to get these massive boats started, then jumping in the basket in the stern of the boat where the tiller and mainsheet are. In almost all of the boats there is a two-man crew: one to steer, and the other to handle the mainsheet and jib if they have one.

Stern-steerers *Ferdinand the Bull* and *Taku* are about 42 feet long and are fierce competitors. Buddy Melges (considered the best sailor in the world on ice and water) owns the *Bull*, and Bill Bentsen (Olympic gold medal winner with Buddy) owns the *Taku*. The mechanical advantage needed to crank in the mainsheet on these boats is enormous. The big boats found that using a ratcheting wheel with a brake used on railroad cars worked really well. The wheel was about the size of a car's steering wheel, and the brake was controlled with a lever.

To understand how it works, picture a crucifix lying face-up. The hull, or fuselage, is the long member, and the plank is the crossmember. Now the mast would be located just forward of the plank. On the ends of the plank are the runners or skates. The runners are around five or six feet long and very sharp so they won't slip sideways on the ice. There is also a runner at the back of the boat attached to the tiller to turn the boat. The crew sits in a basket at the stern.

The mast has a huge downward force when sailing; sometimes this force can push the front of the hull down and lift the stern up. Consequently, the windward plank goes up in the air. If that happens, the steering skate loses contact with the ice, and the boat is on its own. The plank lifts way up, and the boat usually spins around, ejecting the crew with all that centrifugal force. In that situation, it is essential to get away from the six-foot razor-sharp skates. It is easy to prevent this by simply releasing the mainsheet to bring the stern down and then resume steering in the right direction.

During one regatta Peter crewed for Bentsen in one race, then with Buddy in the next. Peter controlled the mainsheet on Bentsen's *Taku* and released the main by simply pushing the brake lever up. When he sailed with Buddy on the *Bull*, the boat started to lift, and Buddy yelled to Peter to release the brake. No matter how hard he tried, the brake would not release. The boat was about ready to go into a spin, and Buddy decided it was time to bail out; he was halfway over when the mainsheet released and she came down and they got control.

What was the problem?

Simple: the brake lever on *Taku* was released by pushing the lever up, and on the *Bull* it was the opposite. Peter figured it out just in time. If she'd gone over, we would have had a wild *Bull* on the loose with razor-sharp runners.

It's hard to beat a summer full of sailing, with the ease of backyard access to your boat and the ability to be on the racecourse in ten minutes. Parking your iceboat in front of your house in the winter and participating in a host of regional iceboating events is also tough to beat. One would think this is an inhospitable place for a couple of boys raised in a tropical climate. But we quickly adapted to the activities, the people, and the serious work ethic. Peter and I love it here.

THE *STEALTH*

She is 38 feet long with a six-foot bowsprit and a total weight of 1,850 pounds. Flat-bottomed, with a rounded bow, carrying a huge mainsail and 1,350-square-foot asymmetrical spinnaker, the A-Scow has been unofficially called the fastest production monohull sailboat in the world.

Stealth is one of the half-dozen or more A-Scows on Pewaukee Lake. Our normal crew is six and consists of: Matt Weber who drives, I handled the mainsheet when I was able and still do upon occasion, Rick Wilfert our tactician, Neil Evans (my son in-law), Tom Beckes, and Jim Rehberger. We race every Sunday during the season and draw a large spectator fleet to watch these magnificent monsters tear around the course at speeds exceeding 20 knots. Our crew has been together for a long time, which is important: a great deal of the success or failure depends on the crew work. There are two boards to operate, running backstays, an array of lines to adjust the travelers, vang, jib sheets, mainsheets, downhaul, outhaul, mast rake, bowsprit, spinnaker sheets — plus, we're always shifting our weight to keep the boat heeled exactly on her lines. It is not a "set it and leave it" boat — we are constantly adjusting everyting for the gusts and dramatic wind shifts we get on the inland lakes. This is critical to performance.

At the two major regattas each year, two dozen boats will show up at one of the lakes big enough to handle the fleet. We sail against major ringers like Olympic Gold-medalist Buddy Melges, Andy Burdick, The Porter Brothers, Olympic-medalist Bill Allen, Gordy Bowers, and a number of other hot shots. It's great to sail against these sailors, even though we have little to no chance of beating them.

What could be better than this kind of racing? The boat sits on an electric lift in front of my house alongside our 26-foot tender. The crew shows up at 1300, rigs the boat, and we're on the starting line at 1400. The race usually takes 90 minutes, and if there's no double-header, we're back on the lift with the cover put on and the sails stowed 20 minutes after the race. After snacks and beer that Ruth has prepared, we head to the yacht club to whine or brag about the wind shift that only we saw. It's hard to beat that kind of racing program.

Now you know why we call Pewaukee the center of the sailing universe.

The Stealth *coming in to a leeward mark rounding on Pewaukee Lake*

PROCYON (1987–1993)

The *Procyon* project was one of the biggest, most expensive, time-consuming, frustrating, and controversial projects I've ever undertaken. It was also the most interesting and fulfilling venture with which I've been involved.

It all started in 1987 when I got concerned about the status of boatbuilding on a worldwide basis. We were already suffering from an economy that was in a mild recession and a new luxury tax that was a killer. I felt that we needed something new and fresh. There was very little innovation among sailboat builders; budgets were tight, and companies were barely able to survive, much less afford research and development. Even styling and interiors had very little change from one model to the next, year after year. Only a few people were trying to design products that were out of the box.

In general the monohull sailboats being built were slow and often difficult to rig and handle; many required more than just ma and pa to sail them safely under difficult conditions. The boats could be uncomfortable for those who found it difficult to live in a world that was angled at 25 degrees. There are very few boats that are comfortable in a big sea, so the trick is to get where you need to go as quickly as possible.

Procyon *under sail for a sunset cruise*

Innovation was the lifeblood of our company and industry. We were doing well despite the economy, so I wanted to try to catalyze the builders and designers with fresh ideas. I noted the factors that I felt were critical to increasing sales and production in the industry. The project, I felt, should do 11 things:

- Increase the speed of the boats by at least 10 percent.
- Make the boats easier to sail with a crew of only two people.
- Make the boats quick and easy to rig with a minimum of crew.
- Decrease the maximum heeling angle to about 10 degrees.
- Increase crew safety by relocating sail control lines from the deck to the cockpit.
- Make it possible to decrease and increase sail area with the push of a button or by pulling on a line common in manual furling systems.
- Incorporate new interior designs that use lightweight materials and create more open space.
- Increase the comfort of the boat when the waves are pounding the hull by adding weight.
- Increase vision when docking or maneuvering.
- Make it easy to lower the mast for passage under low bridges.
- Do all this in a cost-effective vessel that looks like a sailboat with modern styling.

Even though many of these criteria seem to be answered by a catamaran design, I felt it was necessary to achieve them in a monohull. In the late 1980s, most people weren't comfortable in catamarans for a number of reasons, including the remote possibility of turning over and the space required to dock. I had some preconceived ideas for solving some of the problems I outlined, but needed the help of a team that could brainstorm solutions to the others. I really wanted to build a boat to try these ideas out, so raising the capital to do such an experiment was another challenge that had to be overcome.

When I presented this idea to Harken's board of directors, their response was lukewarm. Their reaction disturbed me. I thought the idea would be embraced with enthusiasm. I was disappointed and angry, and it clearly showed. Russ Pyle, a good friend and member of the board, talked to me for over an hour to try to get me to understand that we were running a business and that things were going to be different now that we had investors to consider. They were there to invest and make money. Although Russ made me feel better, I was no less determined to fulfill my dream to build that boat: a fast, comfortable, beautiful monohull that cost no more than a standard-production boat.

Cost was going to be a real challenge, since I did not want to raid the company coffers. I was going to have to raise money to do this project. In order to get support from sponsors and manufacturers of the different components, the project needed a lot of credibility. Our name was well known, and that was a good start. But I was just a hardware maker — not a naval architect, sailmaker, interior designer, or electronics expert — and I had no experience in building big boats. I needed to put a credible team together.

The members of the team needed to be more than experts in their field; they needed to be creative and able to think outside the box. The naval architect was going to be the most critical member; for that role, I needed somebody who'd pushed the limits. I really didn't care if he had ever failed in doing so. That led me to Britt Chance. He was known to be difficult to work with and lacking a sense of humor. One time we were driving together in silence, and I thought I'd try a joke on him. He listened intently, but would not even crack a smile. We continued on in silence for another 15 minutes, when all of a sudden he broke out into laughter and said he got it. I think that was the only time I really heard him laugh. Still, we got along well. He got very involved in the project; in fact, he was a pretty good team member.

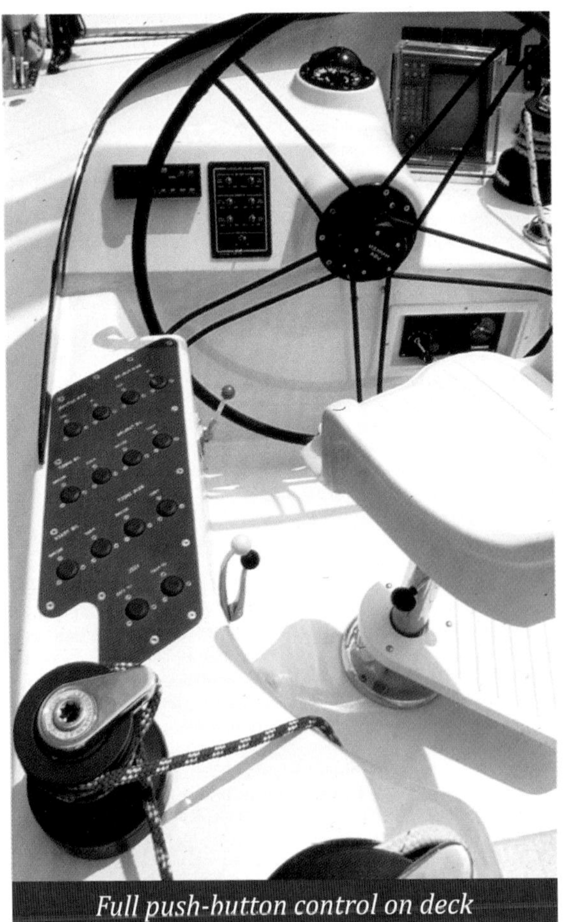

Full push-button control on deck

So what in the world made me consider Britt as my prime candidate?

Dual steering stations ensure the captain always has a clear line of sight

First of all, he was brilliant — not only as a naval architect but also as a physicist. He'd designed a number of winning race boats and was considered one of the top designers in his field. He also had stepped over the edge and designed a few dogs; but I saw his risk-taking as a positive. I asked him if he was interested in joining the team. He wanted to know how much he was going to be paid, and I vaguely told him that we would cover his expenses and see how things went. Before we both agreed, I needed to talk to him about being a member of the team and that it was critical that we did not let egos get in the way. He agreed and we were on our way.

The *Procyon* team:

- Olaf Harken: team leader
- Britt Chance: naval architect; designed *Procyon*, including canting keel
- Diane Attwood: interior designer and stylist
- Art Ellis: Ockum Instruments; supplied navigation and communications electronics
- Charlie Miller: North Sails, Pewaukee loft; supplied sails
- Eric Hall: Hall Spars; supplied spars

- Harken Inc.: supplied hardware and financing
- Frank Butler: Catalina Yachts owner; assembled the hull, deck, and interior
- Windship: built hull and deck
- Milwaukee School of Engineering: designed and built the hydraulic keel canting system.
- O.H. Rodgers: yacht designer, builder, and the guy who could solve problems
- Peter Wilson: project manager
- Russ Pyle: patent and general attorney
- Bill Read: Bank One president; financing
- Amoco Chemical Company: main sponsor; advertising and publicity
- Randy West: our captain extraordinaire

In addition, 44 other companies provided materials and equipment to the project. Almost everything was donated or heavily discounted. Of course, this was still a very expensive project: it was budgeted to be a little over $1 million and turned out to be closer to $2 million.

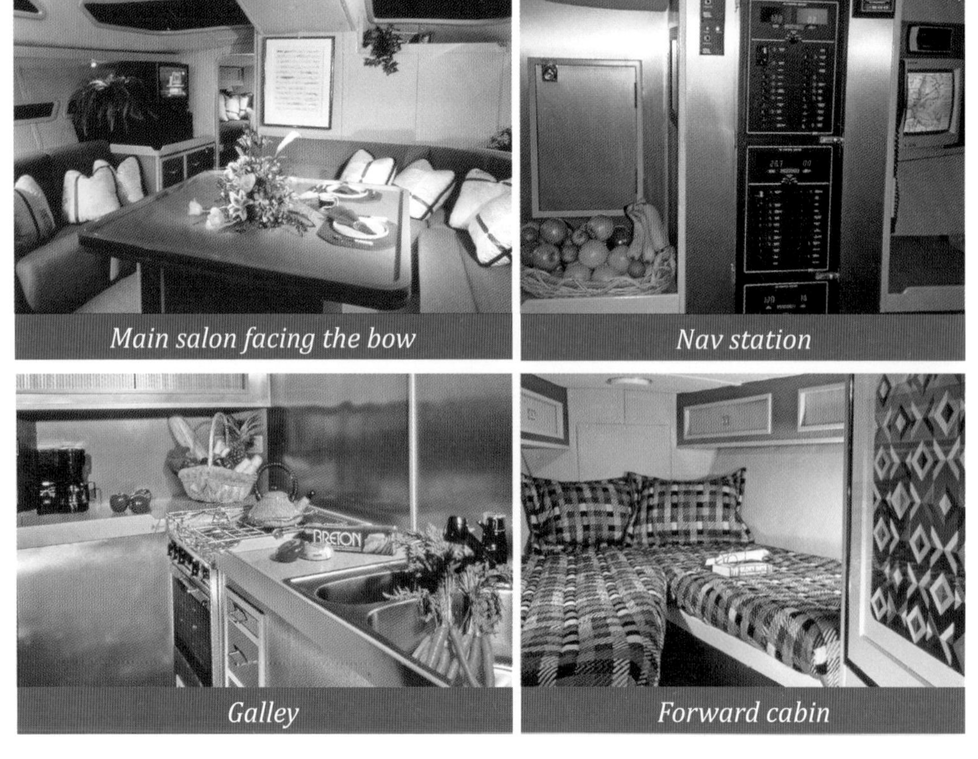

Main salon facing the bow

Nav station

Galley

Forward cabin

Diane Attwood had never designed the interior of a sailing yacht. She was a sailor and had designed the interior of a beautiful 125-foot motor yacht named *Time*. It had a modern and futuristic look instead of the traditional wood interior. She was perfect for the job; I was delighted that she not only accepted the challenge but was enthusiastic and a great team member. We needed fresh ideas, and she had them. She not only helped me out by donating her work to the project, but was able to come up with great modern and lightweight solutions.

Charlie Miller managed the North Sails loft in Pewaukee. We'd shared a building with him since our earliest days in business, and he was one of our closest friends. Charlie had no choice: how could he stand by while another sailmaker was involved? The North Sails management group agreed to make the sails as their contribution — a major donation. Charlie designed and made the sails using Kevlar® for both the main and the jib. It was not an easy project, since the main had to furl like the jib and have a decent shape when partially furled between the two legs of the bipod mast.

Electronics expert Art Ellis manager of Ockum Instruments, owned by Dick Purdy, supplied instrumentation to most of the America's Cup yachts. They had some unusual features such as magnetic strips that could be attached to any one

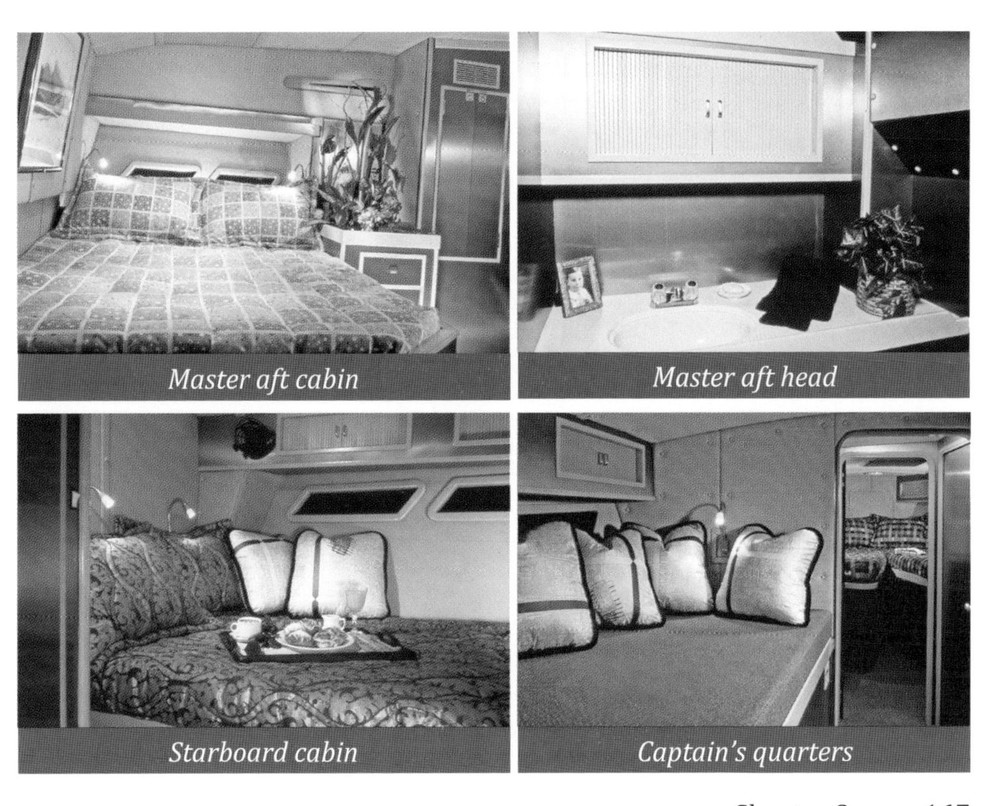

Master aft cabin

Master aft head

Starboard cabin

Captain's quarters

of the digital displays on the bridge. If you wanted apparent wind, you just stuck that strip to the display and it changed the readout to apparent wind. Their system supplied all the different data to universal receptacles — a breakthrough idea in its day. Art also had to integrate the brand-new MapTech GPS software into the system that was donated by Gary Comer, the Lands' End founder who back in 1968 convinced Peter and me to put our family name on the hardware business. It was an amazing system at the time. We relied on it in many cases when we had to do some tricky night maneuvering in storms with no visibility and through narrow passages in rivers or reefs. Today that system is common technology, but it had a wow factor then.

Eric Hall of Hall Spars built the bipod mast designed by Dirk Kramer. It was a first, and one of the major visible differences of the yacht. Amoco Chemical donated the carbon that was paramount to keeping the mast's weight down. The mast was a real challenge and had its ups and downs — pun intended.

Gary Carlin of Windship Custom Yachts of Tampa, Florida, built the molds and the hull and deck, using a mixture of fiberglass, carbon, and Kevlar®. He vacuum-bagged the laminates to create a strong and light boat. Frank Butler, owner of Catalina Yachts, took on the job of putting the hull and deck together. They did all of the joinery work and installed all the interior materials used in Diane's design. The hull and deck were trucked from Windship in the middle of the night to the Catalina Yard in Largo, Florida, 20 miles away. It was quite a spectacle.

O.H. Rodgers was critical in the process. There were plenty of questions and problems to solve every day: a lot of what we were doing had never been done before, and someone had to come up with the solution right then and there. Using his years of experience as a boatbuilder, designer, and practical engineer, Rodgers kept the project moving whenever the builders were stuck. He later designed a new keel with a much shallower draft that performed better than the deep-draft keel.

Randy West responded to our ad for a captain and quickly became our choice from the many applicants. We needed a very capable, licensed captain who would also be our public-relations leader. The boat had many events to attend for Amoco Chemical and numerous boat shows, races, and charters, and constant crowds of curious people wanted to come aboard or ask questions.

With astronomy being one of my hobbies, I named the boat *Procyon*. Amoco *Procyon* was launched in 1991, then immediately made the rounds of boat

Procyon *magazine coverage*

shows in Newport, Annapolis, Miami, Fort Lauderdale, and St. Petersburg. Long lines of people waited to board her at the different shows; we estimated she was visited by as many as 10,000 people. CEOs of big companies and famous people sailed her, including the Secretary of Commerce Bus Mosbacher and Wisconsin governor Tommy Thompson. Some officials at the places we visited even wanted us to dock where we could bring attention to their waterfront.

Interviews with the press were requested by *Popular Science*, *Time*, *Business Week*, *Fortune*, the *New York Times*, and trade magazines in hydraulics, carbon fibers, navigation, as well as just about every sailing magazine around the world in every language. When I was not available, Randy was our front man for all of this. He not only answered their questions but entertained them with a litany of sea stories and jokes. Randy never tired of this and managed to also entertain quite a few lovely ladies along the way. As a sailor, he quickly gained the confidence of the passengers and crew. He could fix most problems, was strict about safety procedures, and handled inclement weather without panic. He was a captain extraordinaire.

Results of the Experiment

The purpose of the *Procyon* project was to try new ideas and see which were viable. Although we intended to patent some of them, we had no intention of selling them to legitimate builders or naval architects. We felt the payback would be an increase in boat sales that would help to revive our industry. Our innovations were by no means the best or only solutions but a catalyst to inspire creative thinking.

Procyon brought forth many innovations including the bipod mast, ease of handling, ability to decrease or increase sail area, the modernized interior, the water-ballast system, the exterior styling, dual steering stations that were unconventionally located towards the forward center of the boat, and finally the canting-keel performance — along with the method of making and installing this system. Complete push-button sailing was located and duplicated at both steering stations. There was even a system for getting a physically disabled person on the boat that would allow them freedom to move around on and below the deck.

The Bipod Mast

Procyon's two-legged mast was one of the boat's most distinctive features. The mast was an A-frame with two 90-foot, airfoil-shaped tubes made of carbon fiber and the mainsail and jib were on a roller-furling system which could be hydraulic, electric, or manual.

Procyon's *bipod mast*

The theory behind the bipod was simple. On conventional sailboats, a jib is more efficient than a mainsail because it has a clean entry into the wind. The bipod allowed the mainsail to enter the wind cleanly, with nothing more than a furling foil on the leading edge. Wind-tunnel tests have shown that one wire can create as much turbulence as an airfoil-shaped tube whose diameter is 10 times greater than that of the wire.

The bipod performed very well when the boat was matched against boats like the Santa Cruz 70s where she could hold her own upwind. The lighter, longer 70s were definitely faster off the wind. Still, it was difficult to isolate the cause, since other factors like the canting keel had a large influence on performance.

Unfortunately the mast was our nemesis and had a great deal to do with the failure of our primary objectives because it came crashing down twice. Its airfoil design wouldn't stop sailing at the dock or at anchor and the mechanical fastening systems were not strong enough.

The first mast came down in 1992. The 90-pound assembly holding the two pods together had a galvanic battle going on between the stainless screws and the aluminum assembly — the fittings corroded and failed. Up to this point the boat was on a roll, being sailed a lot and doing its job of testing new ideas and exposing them to the public and the marine industry. This totally avoidable accident put the boat out of commission at a huge cost. It took 14 months to get the boat back to Rhode Island and have a new mast built. It threw the project so far behind that it lost all momentum.

Showing off under sail

The second mast had a newly designed top assembly — stainless-steel sockets to contain the mast this time. There was still a problem though: the airfoil pods wanted to sail all the time. This should have been corrected but was not. When the boat was at the dock, it would heel over as much as 20 degrees.

The second mast failed in Miami in 1993. There was a sudden storm with peak winds over 100 mph. The boat heeled over excessively next to a piling on the dock that was right where the mast attached to the gunwale area. The heeling kept the starboard pod banging into the piling until it finally broke through and cracked the mast. Several minutes later it snapped and came down, bringing the port pod with it.

We completely redesigned the third mast. She was about 8 feet shorter with pods that came closer together at the top. The final mast brought the pods together with an assembly that weighed only 22 pounds. The original 90-pound top assemblies on the first two masts had negated the advantages of using carbon. The airfoil shape was changed to a more elliptical one so it wouldn't sail all the time. The wall thickness was increased, and backing plates were used behind all fittings attached to the carbon. She took a lot of abuse and proved very successful.

We lost two years of sailing between the mast failures, and they had a devastating impact on the project. We learned a lot from the three masts, but felt more experimentation was necessary before it could be made practical for a boat builder — even though we felt the third mast was getting close.

The Canting Keel

Of all *Procyon's* features, the canting keel was the most successful, with one exception. The exception is that today the technology is only used by a small group of specialized racing boats like those in the Volvo Ocean Race and still isn't being used in production. The primary reason is that builders have not been presented with a package deal and a source with which they feel comfortable.

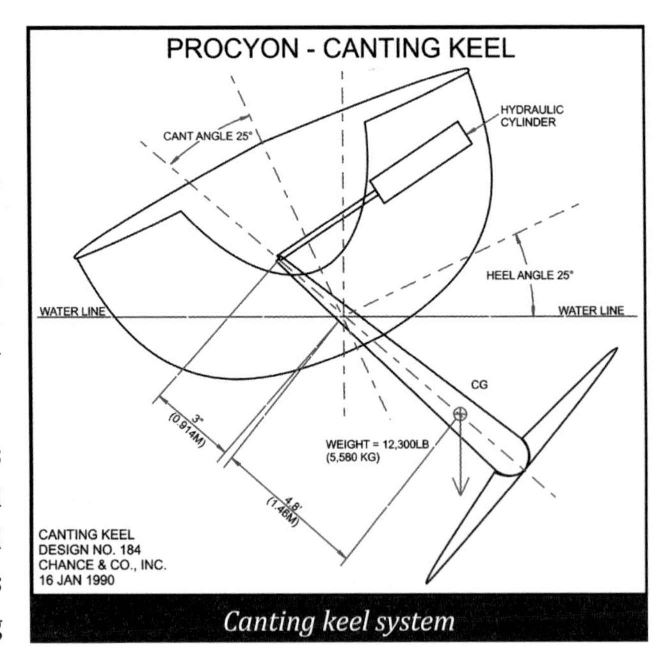

Canting keel system

Van Alan Clark, a famous East Coast sailor and officer of the International Yacht Racing Union, was the first to use a canting keel on his 40-footer in 1980, *Red Herring*. It incorporated a large watertight box in the interior, with the keel controlled by a block and tackle to swing it from side to side.

The system on *Procyon* was much easier to install and operate and was perfectly viable in cost and simplicity. *Procyon* was the perfect platform to test a new system, since the Milwaukee School of Engineering is the foremost center for fluid-power studies in the United States and is in our backyard. Steve Whiting, who designed the hydraulic system, was a dean there and specialized in fluid-power. Britt Chance came up with the idea and used David Greely of Atlantic Applied Research to help design the keel shape. David's other design work was on submarine shapes, so he had the computer power to model the different shapes. Britt also had to design a system capable of hitting a rock at 11 knots, which he deemed to be a reasonable number. This was tested several times inadvertently, and his calculations were correct.

The keel on *Procyon* was originally 11 feet long and had an 8-foot wing on the end made of cast iron. The wing at the bottom of the keel eliminated the need for the separate foil towards the bow used in the current designs of racing boats. To cant the keel, a push-pull hydraulic ram was attached to the arm welded to the keel.

It was simple and extremely effective. Moving the 13,000-pound wing keel to 35 degrees was like putting 17 people on the rail. It was invisible in the cabin, unless you slid back a maintenance panel. The keel allowed for more sail area — which all translated to comfort and speed. In a tacking duel, we would simply

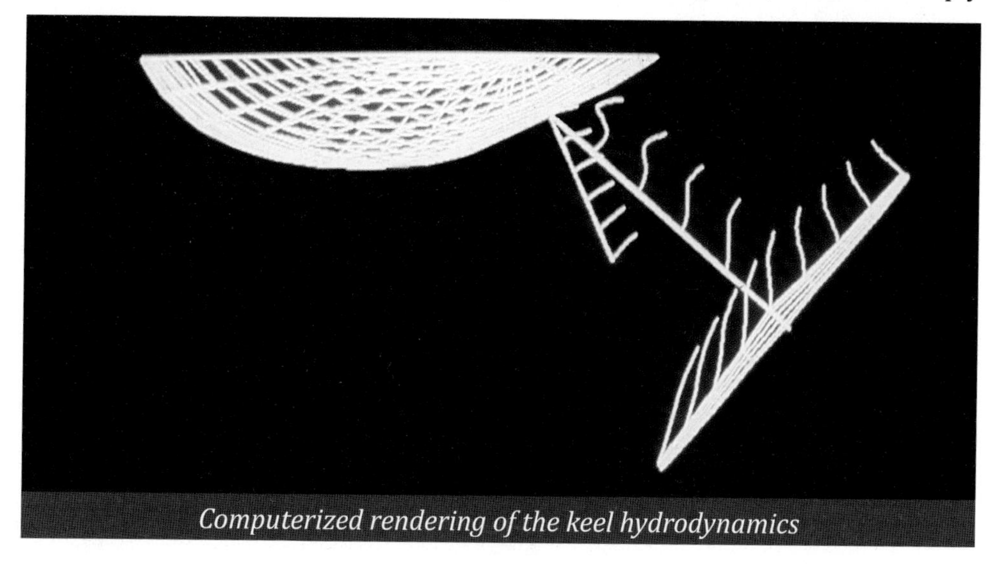

Computerized rendering of the keel hydrodynamics

Underneath Procyon

open the keel valves in the cockpit, and the keel would drop under gravity; we'd then close the valves, which locked the keel into the new high side. It was similar to the efficient roll tack that dinghy sailors use.

Our pointing abilities with the wing were excellent: we could out-point a Santa Cruz 70 and many other boats with fin keels. The ability to tip the boat also made boarding easier, and made it possible to flatten the boat under sail while the galley was in use or people were below. We even used it to tilt the boat to get under a few bridges where we needed an extra foot or two of clearance.

The 11-foot draft was a problem. We hit the bottom so many times, I thought of putting wheels on the wings. It was something that seriously needed to change. O.H. Rodgers designed a new 7-foot keel using the existing structure; it

A view of the keel just after construction and before launch

worked beautifully and only changed the ability to correct the heeling angle by 5 degrees. This opened up many new places including the Erie Canal. The second canting keel was an A-plus.

My dream is to install a canting keel on a production boat to demonstrate the performance, minimum loss of interior space, cost effectiveness, and the solution to eliminating the one or two separate foils ahead of the keel that are fairly fragile. The builders haven't done it since they are not familiar with nor do they have a source for the system we successfully tested on *Procyon*.

I would have pursued this project further if I could have found the time and a builder willing to work with me. It could revolutionize designs and be the most effective gain in performance since the carbon-fiber mast.

Adventures with **Procyon**

When christening and launching a boat, I heard it was bad luck to fail to break the champagne bottle when hitting it over the bow. Ruth had heard this, too, and since she had the honor of breaking the bottle for the launching of *Procyon*, she made sure it was going to break. Her stance and look of determination reminded me of Babe Ruth getting ready to hit a home run. She smacked that bottle so hard that glass and champagne flew out over 30 feet and doused and cut some of our guests, including one of the big shots from Amoco. Hitting the bow too hard also seems to be a sign of bad luck. But no one was seriously cut, and soon people started to laugh, and we had a great time.

Almost everyone in our core group was there in Tampa for the christening, along with friends, families, and the press. We later stepped the mast, rigged the sails, and took her out for a maiden voyage in light-to-moderate breezes.

On our initial leg from Tampa to Key West, one morning I looked out the window of the starboard forward cabin, which was a little below the waterline, and saw an amazing sight: a pod of dolphins swimming alongside above and below the water. It appeared that they were looking at me looking at them. What a way to wake up — seeing them on our first voyage.

The initial performance was excellent and after some sea trials, we were ready to begin the voyage from Tampa to Chicago. The schedule for the boat was to sail her to Chicago via the St. Lawrence River where we would do multiple day trips with the Amoco people, friends, family, and contributors to the project.

The Chicago-to-Mackinac Race

By the time *Procyon* was delivered to Chicago, she was ready to be tested in a major race to see if the performance met the criteria. The Chicago-to-Mackinac race is one of the major races in the world circuit, with about 300 boats entered. It starts in Chicago and finishes 330 miles north at Mackinac Island at the top of the Great Lakes.

Procyon did not have a rating and had multiple features, such as the canting keel and pushbutton controls, that were not allowed. We had asked the race organizers from the Chicago Yacht Club if we could race along with the other boats in the large-boat division. They agreed, and in addition we had the world-famous Gary Jobson skippering the boat. Gary is a collegiate champion who has sailed and won in several grand-prix events, including Ted Turner's winning team in the America's Cup. He also is a commentator for ESPN Sports TV channel during the America's Cup. With a small crew of six (as compared to the average crews on these big boats of 17 sailors) we wanted to see if we could easily manage the boat and use our keel to even things up.

We started in a tight reach with the wind coming from the northwest and held our own against the Santa Cruz 70s, hot racing boats referred to as "sleds." The wind shifted to the southeast and freshened up, so we put up the spinnaker. Since this was their optimum sailing angle, we could not hold on to the sleds, but we were close. The wind increased, and we were pushing the limits of our light-air spinnaker. It blew up, and Gary requested we put up another chute. We said we didn't have another one, and he was shocked to be on a racing boat without different sails for different wind conditions. So we got to work sewing and taping along the tear in our one chute; after three hours, we'd sort of repaired it. The sleds were long gone. By now the wind shifted in our favor, so we didn't need the chute. With the boat close-hauled, we were really smoking, and our keel was doing its job. We could finally see one of the sleds and tacked at Gray's Reef Lighthouse for the sprint to the finish. We ended up sixth; the only boats to beat us were the four sleds and a big 80-foot race boat. We felt pretty good, considering the setback of the tear in the spinnaker.

In addition to the Mackinac Race, *Procyon* was entered in the Fort Lauderdale to Key West Race, Antigua Race Week, and the Queens Cup across Lake Michigan. When going from one venue to another, different crews helped Randy West sail her.

Procyon at Sea

Weather was always a big issue, since the boat was on a tight schedule and frequently had to sail through difficult conditions in order to get to where she was going on time. Randy was very skilled and was very cautious about making sure that there was a good plan for a man overboard and that people wore lifejackets when the weather was inclement. A rogue wave swept over the entire boat once when she was on a trip going south in the Atlantic, and we would have lost a man if he hadn't been tethered to the boat. Another time when Randy was not on board, we were delivering the boat from Norfolk to Fort Lauderdale in moderately heavy weather. The wind was forecast to increase to as much as 40 knots but would shift from the northeast to the north. We had to round Cape Hatteras before the shift so we'd be protected by land.

The forecast was wrong, however, and the wind continued to come from the northeast, meaning that we would not get the protection from land. The waves were building to 10 feet, with some at 15 feet. Syd Millman, a friend and coworker at Harken, had experience steering in big waves, so he and I took turns and changed every half hour. My daughter Heidi was on this leg of the trip with us, but because of the conditions, I had her stay below. At one point the boat broached when a big gust came through. Heidi had been sleeping in the aft cabin and woke up plastered against the opposing wall then slowly slid down to the floor as the boat righted. After almost 10 hours of steering in these heavy seas, we decided that we could not make our next stop without some relief.

The nearest port was Wilmington, North Carolina, 20 miles up the Cape Fear River. We had to go 20 miles around Frying Pan Shoals and could hear the surf breaking over the shoals. It was pitch black, and we had to find the entrance to the river. We followed the GPS system and sighed with relief when we saw the red buoy on our starboard just like the MapTech charts showed.

We then went over 20 miles up the river with lots of bends at night with howling wind and rain but calm seas. When we reached Wilmington, we saw an open space behind a Coast Guard Ship and docked. It was 3 a.m.

At around 9 a.m. we were awakened by a lot of talking and figured the Coast Guard didn't like our parking place. On the contrary, there was a crowd of civilians and Coast Guard personnel all gawking at our boat. A Coast Guard officer asked us where we came from, and we said we had come up the river after having left Annapolis two days ago. He laughed and said there was no way we could have come up the river that night with the weather like it was. We told him to come aboard and see the MapTech System. Ours was the second one ever made. He was in awe and said they had nothing like it aboard their ship and wondered why a civilian yacht should have a better system than the Coast Guard.

We soon had a string of people come aboard to see the boat, including the mayor. After a tour he asked us if we would dock at the end of the main street coming down to the river at the center of town. We obliged him and left the boat under the care of Bonnie Chase, one of my longtime friends from college. The boat ended up being used as the main photo of a postcard for Wilmington. We came back two weeks later for the next leg of the trip. We needed extra crew, so we picked up a couple that said they were seasoned sailors. After another harrowing night of weather, they became very seasick and we had to take refuge in Saint Augustine to drop them off.

On to Milwaukee, **Procyon's** *New Home*

There were lots of good and memorable times on the travels of *Procyon*. I was not on many of them since I had to work and only joined the boat when I could.

After several mishaps with the rig, and taking into account the extravagant costs of docking and maintaining the 65-foot yacht, we ultimately decided to bring her to Milwaukee, where she would be in fresh water and be only a half-hour drive away for me to work and sail on. In the winter she would go into inside storage with no worries.

The trip from Annapolis to Milwaukee at the end of her saltwater journey was truly memorable. Washington, DC, was only an hour's drive from Annapolis, so I took my daughters Heather and Heidi and their boyfriends to visit the many sights of our capital including the Senate in debate, the Vietnam Wall, the Lincoln Memorial, and the Treasury Department where they were printing up money in copious quantities. A day later we left for New York, where we had a reserved docking space beneath the Twin Towers at the exclusive North Cove Marina for free since they really wanted the boat as an attraction.

Ruth and my daughter Hilary joined us in New York, and we had a great time with the best location in the city, though it wasn't very private. As we sat in the cockpit for a cocktail in the evenings with the beautiful World Trade Center as a background, or got up early in the morning, there was always a group of people looking at the boat. We visited museums, the NBC Studios, and saw the Broadway production of *Cats* before we left to go up the Hudson River to Albany.

Procyon *cruising downwind*

The trip up the Hudson River was easy, until we ran aground near Poughkeepsie, where about a dozen markers got us confused and there was no GPS signal to guide us. We backed off and freed ourselves and decided to drop the anchor in order to figure it all out. The markers made some sense, since there were several inlets merging into the river, so we tried to take off and give it a try. But the anchor was hooked on something, and we couldn't break loose. A tow boat came out, and after several attempts branches started coming out of the water about 100 feet around us. As our luck would have it, we had hooked the anchor on a very old and large oak tree at the bottom of the river. The skipper cut the anchor and charged us $300 for his efforts. I was pretty sure he retrieved the anchor after we left. It was getting dark, and the river was very difficult to make out.

A large tugboat went by, so we radioed the skipper and asked if he would mind if we followed him. He said, "Glad to," and we had a peaceful ride to the Scarano Boat Yard at Albany. The Scarano team was great and fashioned a set of stands on which to set the huge 90-foot A-frame mast on the deck. They gently lowered the mast down with one of their tall cranes attached to a harness, and it settled into the stands. *Procyon* was 65 feet, so we had 20 feet protruding from the bow and 15 feet sticking out from the transom. We were now driving a 90-footer.

The next stop was the Albany Yacht Club, where we provisioned and got tips on traversing the Erie Canal. As we left the pier, we still had not become accustomed to our new length, and our stern wiped out a string of lamps on the dock. Whoops! We offered to pay for them, but they insisted it was out of the question. Nice folks. I think they were worried about more damage if we tried to stop.

Before entering the canal, we picked up a dozen or so bales of hay to protect our topsides from the crusty sides of the ditch and then started the fun journey. Most of the locks were operated with one man who would open the sluice gates at one lock and then jump into his truck to meet us at the next lock. We planned to stay overnight at Lock Number 11, which was in Amsterdam, New York. It was the 4th of July, and they had parked a barge in a wide spot for shooting off fireworks. We thought we'd better move on, but they invited us to come to the main dock and tie up. Pretty soon we had a long line of people coming aboard, including the mayor, police chief, and fire chief. They assured us the fireworks were going to go away from us so we had front row seats for the show. It was a great evening with a crowd of folks all over the boat.

To clear some of the very low bridges we had taped a stick with a tennis ball to the front of the bipod mast as it lay on the deck. If the ball didn't clear the bridge, we had to stop. By tipping the boat over with the canting keel we were able to clear some bridges by inches. After reaching Buffalo and getting the mast up, we went from Lake Ontario to Lake Erie, which were separated by Niagara Falls. Going over the Falls didn't seem like a good idea, so we went into the huge Welland Locks used by the big ships and felt like a minnow in a big river.

We had a great trip up the Hudson and Erie Canal to the Great Lakes. The Milwaukee Yacht Club was anxious to have *Procyon* out front.

The Fire

Besides the mast crashing down twice, one other really horrible thing happened with the boat. There was a terrible fire that did major damage and almost killed my daughter and two of her friends.

Just weeks after arriving in Milwaukee, my daughter Heidi and two of her friends were staying on board on a hot summer night to get the boat ready for a sail with a dozen guests on Saturday. They hadn't seen each other all summer, so they sat outside and talked until about 2 a.m. before going to bed. Heidi was in the large aft cabin, and the girls were in the forward cabins with the hatches closed since the air conditioner was on. Since they got in late, they didn't open the boat and take the padlocks off the hatches. The hatch in the aft cabin was locked from the outside with a padlock where Heidi was.

Around 4 a.m. the phone rang in our house in Pewaukee. Heidi was calling from the satellite phone because she smelled smoke. I told her to get the girls up and off the boat. She instructed them to go to the dockmaster and call 911. We then tried to find the source while talking to her over the phone. She said the smoke was coming through light fixtures in the overhead of the main salon. I was telling her to check the engine compartment, battery storage, electric panel, and to turn off the main power switch, when all of a sudden I heard her scream and then the phone went dead. (This was before cell phones were popular).

Ruth and I called 911, then threw some clothes on and raced toward Milwaukee, arriving about 25 minutes later. There were 10 fire trucks on the scene; they'd pieced together about 700 feet of hose to reach the boat, since she was at the end of the face dock. To our delight, we saw the three girls, and Heidi explained that the main salon had burst into flames. She'd gone up the companion way after letting out a scream as the hydraulics all turned on and almost pulled the mast down. She fell going back through the hatch to turn the main switch off for the hydraulics before escaping the flames. Since the satellite phone was hardwired in, she couldn't take it with her. If she had not woken up, she would not have been able to get out with the hatch padlocked and the other girls could have been killed by smoke. We were so relieved that they were safe. The two girls were fine and Heidi only had a sprained ankle from the fall.

The damage to the boat was extensive and not worth trying to fix her. The main salon was a charred black hole, and the rest of the inside was badly damaged by smoke. The big wraparound window and other windows had all either melted from the immense heat or been broken with axes by the firemen to get them open to put the fire out. The fire had been caused by a short in the connection to the shore power, which had been hit by lightning earlier in the week.

So we said our goodbyes and turned her over to the insurance company. They sold her to a broker for a song. It was a sad loss and a terrible end for our baby, but there was still some life in her. A company specializing in renovation bought her and spent over a million dollars building a whole new interior. The mast was fine, the engine was good, the hydraulic systems just needed new hoses, and the deck above the salon needed to be strengthened. Two Frenchmen bought her; then due to a falling out between them, they did nothing with the boat and she sat in a canal in Ft. Lauderdale for several years. I know she has changed hands a number of times but has seldom been out sailing. I had considered buying her back from them or starting over, but it was time to say goodbye and turn my attention back to the company.

TEAM ADVENTURE (2001)

It was a cold day in Wisconsin near the end of March 2001 when I received a call via satellite phone. It was from Cam Lewis, in the middle of the Atlantic Ocean, sailing for Marseilles. Cam was on the last leg to finishing The Race. This was a race around the world in a "no rules" sailboat: any kind, any shape, any dimension. The only restriction was that the boat had to keep the world's five great capes to port: Cape Leeuwin, (southeast Australia), Cape Froward (South America), Cape Agulhas (South Africa), Southeast Cape (Tasmania), and Southwest Cape (New Zealand) — no going through any canals, and lots of Southern Ocean sailing. The Southern Ocean, stretching 7,000 uninterrupted miles around Antarctica, is home to some of the world's stormiest conditions. It can produce huge waves and freezing temperatures.

There were four huge catamarans built for The Race. Each was designed purely for speed, with just enough strength to stay together around the course. Cam Lewis commanded the 110-foot catamaran *Team Adventure*. His team had been leading the first leg of The Race, going at full-throttle into the Southern Ocean, when a huge wave damaged a cross beam, one of the essential structural components that keeps the hulls together and supports the mast. The crew had to divert to Cape Town, where a shore crew made repairs. Of course, when they got going again they were several days behind their competitors, but one of the four boats had already dropped out. And in those brutal conditions, the *Team Adventure* crew knew anything was possible. Though they ultimately came in third, they'd caught up quite a distance before the finish.

With The Race now almost behind him, Cam was calling to ask if I'd join the crew to sail from Spain to the U.S. East Coast via San Salvador in the Bahamas — the island where Columbus first made landfall in the New World. I talked to Ruth, and she gave her blessing; she knew it was something I had really wanted to do.

It took about a minute for me to make the call. I was on the way.

On April 5, I arrived in Mallorca, where *Team Adventure* was docked. For the first time, I saw the island's mountains to the north and the many farm fields with vacation resorts on the coastal areas. Hundreds

Team Adventure *under sail during The Race*

Preparing to raise the sails after the repairs

of small Dutch-style windmills dotted the valleys. Palma itself sprawled through hilly terrain on the island's west coast. *Team Adventure* was docked at Puerto Portals, a beautiful Mediterranean marina filled with luxury yachts.

My first impression of *Team Adventure* was that she was big — until you went below. I could see straightaway that our accommodations would be pretty tight. We would definitely know who was wearing what cologne. I took my place in the starboard hull, where eight of us shared six pipe berths, a tiny head, and a galley sink. There was some storage space but not much. Our plan was to take watches; that meant that no more than four or five people would be below at any one time.

The next day, a truck pulled up in the morning with our provisions. We sorted out foul-weather and safety gear, stowed our belongings, and loaded the provisions. There was no refrigeration, so the shopping team needed to be creative. We took on fresh food for about three days: lots of apples and oranges, as well as canned and dry foods. Our cook would turn these ingredients into gourmet meals even after the fresh lettuce turned brown. Ironically, we ate out of dog bowls with sporks — dog bowls are economical with a non-slip rubber ring on the bottom, and a very practical solution to keeping plates on the table. And if you haven't seen a spork before, it's a fork and spoon combined into one utensil.

Our fancy dog bowl dishes

We then installed *Team Adventure's* repaired mainsail — a six-hour job, given the sail's massive size. We put in the battens and lashed each attachment point to the Harken Battcar system.

On the following day, we left around noon for our practice sail. Those of us coming from smaller boats were surprised to learn that every maneuver took about three times as long as you would expect. *Team Adventure* was just that enormous. Take the basic maneuver of hoisting a new headsail. We had this headsail called "the Mule" that could carry up to about 20 knots of breeze. It had a 140-foot hoist with the halyard on a 3:1 purchase, making the distance actually 420 feet. After 15 minutes and 12 people rotating in on 6 grinder positions, finally the thing would reach the top. The simplest operations were a real chore!

Taking turns on the winch to hoist the main

The massive main sail on Team Adventure

Cam Lewis has made a lot of friends on his journeys around the world, and he made two of them in Palma. One was the port captain at the marina who gave him free docking; the other was an elderly gentleman, an avid sailor who owns several serious yachts. Cam invited both of them to join us for our practice sail off Palma, and they enjoyed themselves immensely. They each brought wine to the boat, about 60 bottles in total of great Spanish wines. They were stored under Ken Brown's bunk, which was the lowest of the three-stack where I was located.

With a few guests aboard and our green crew, we raised the Solent (the large foresail), laid off the boat about 40 degrees from the wind, and let her go. In about 12 knots of breeze we went quickly up to 20 knots of boatspeed, and in the gusts we exceeded 25.

It's hard to say in words what a thrill it is to sail at speeds over 25 knots. What a machine! We tacked and jibed about eight times and put in the first reef for practice. It wasn't as difficult as I expected, although the conditions were ideal. Doing it at night in a gale on a bouncing trampoline with a fire hose in your face would be a different story.

We plotted our passage at a little over 4,500 miles, and expected to average between 300 and 600 miles a day unless we lost the wind. Our route would take us through the Straits of Gibraltar and south past the Canary Islands, where we hoped to catch the easterly trade winds. At 23 degrees north, about the latitude of the Tropic of Cancer, we planned to turn west toward San Salvador in the Bahamas. From there, we'd sail either through or around the Bahamas to catch the Gulf Stream and head north to Savannah, Georgia, our destination. We expected the trip to take between 10 and 16 days. In order to use apparent wind to multiply our speed as an iceboat does, we hoped to set a course that would take us 45 degrees away from our rhumb line.

On the third day, we began our voyage. Our first passage from Mallorca to Gibraltar was upwind most of the way. Shortly after leaving Mallorca, we were slamming into the waves so hard that we had to slow it down. It sounded like the boat was coming apart when we went below. That first night when we went to sleep, we had to put pillows behind our heads to keep from slamming into the bulkheads every time we hit a wave.

After leaving Gibraltar and the Mediterranean behind us, we sailed just south of west in a 15- to 20-knot northerly breeze. The waves off the coast of Africa were 15 to 20 feet high, but they were smooth, rolling ocean swells. *Team Adventure* averaged between 20 and 22 knots in those conditions.

Gibraltar was impressive. We passed through the straits in the early evening, keeping the northern shore about a mile off. The northern side is British

Passing the Rock of Gibraltar

Messaging home via satellite email

(Gibraltar is a British territory). On the southern side of the seven-mile-wide straits is "Hercules Gate," part of the Atlas Mountains of Morocco — a magnificent sight. We encountered a lot of shipping traffic through the Straits of Gibraltar. Having run out of breeze and with a lot of current, we decided to motor through to avoid creating any problems with the shipping.

In those first couple of days of the passage we experienced no problems, other than getting the satellite email communications system running to send email and photos directly from the boat to friends and schools around the world. Since we were following the voyage of Christopher Columbus, several schools in the US and UK followed along for history and geography.

After our first days at sea, I sent this report back home from *Team Adventure*: "The power and responsiveness of this cat are phenomenal. Compared to other catamarans, I was a bit surprised to see how well she points, having sailed upwind through most of the Mediterranean. She takes waves so well — you can't even feel 3- and 4-footers. We're following a watch schedule of 4 hours on and 4 hours off during the night and 6 hours on and 6 hours off during the day."

By noon on April 11, we were in our groove, sailing southbound at 17 knots, with a 22-knot breeze off the port bow in 7-foot seas. We sailed *Team Adventure* in a way that was familiar to me from iceboating: in a narrow groove relative to the wind to obtain maximum apparent wind, and therefore speed. Unfortunately that meant our groove was either due west or due south, while our destination was to the southwest. In order to avoid parking in mid-Atlantic doldrums for several days, we had to get to about 19 degrees south, another 400 miles. But averaging a speed of 17 knots over 18 hours took out some of the sting.

Surfing along at 17 knots

Following the advice of the New Hampshire-based weather gurus at Commanders Weather, we dug down deep and continued south before making our hard right-hand turn for the Bahamas. Commanders continually gave us a set of recommended waypoints to avoid bad weather and the doldrums. Through this stretch, we really ate up the miles, covering more than 400 miles in 24 hours.

What a crew we had aboard for this passage: 15 people, all from different backgrounds, nationalities, sexes, jobs, and ages. (Having crossed the 60th meridian, I was in the old-man category). Among us were professional sailors, two teachers, seven guests, a PR man, and Cam's dad, George Lewis. Our professional guys were Frazier Brown and Hugh Piggins from New Zealand and Tom Gonzales from Miami. The guests were Tom Yale from Yale Cordage; Ross Sherbrooke, an old friend of the Lewis family; Betsy Allison, an Olympic sailor; Jim McCarthy, a hot Tornado sailor; Trevor Baylis, a 49er sailor and windsurfer hotshot; Peter Johnstone from the Escape Boat Company (and, later, the founder of Gunboat Catamarans); two teachers: Susie Rieck from Wisconsin, who would report to the schools on a daily basis, and Janet Bradley, a South African who teaches in England; and myself. We all got along fine together — lots of laughs and cooperation — there were no whiners.

Our big physical exercise, besides grinding winches, was jumping up and down on the huge trampoline — 40 feet from side to side and about 60 feet fore and aft — that joined the hulls. Watching people cross between hulls inspired us to plan a contest for some time later, in calmer seas, in which we could judge for style, creativity, and comedy. One thing about the boat life on the off-watch: I didn't have any problems sleeping. During my watch, I got quite a workout at all positions on the boat! There is always work to be done.

Having some fun jumping on the trampoline

Playing boatball

Cam was a great teacher of how to jibe and tack this boat safely. Each maneuver began with a small meeting beforehand to make sure everyone knew his or her assignment. With loads of 10 tons on a sheet, we needed to practice extreme care to prevent injury to the crew and boat. For this part of the passage, every maneuver involved three sails: a gennaker, a staysail, and the huge mainsail.

To tack or jibe, we first needed to center the mainsail traveler. Two backstays needed to be released and brought forward. Two winches on the new high side needed to be connected together to pull in the gennaker sheet, and one winch needed to be made ready to trim the main. The staysail sheet needed to be tied off, and then we were ready with one person on the new leeward side to release the gennaker at just the right time to avoid serious damage. Cam would make the turn when our speed was at absolute maximum; that eased the pressure off the sails in the turn. Then, for what seemed like hours, four people would grind like mad to haul in the big gennaker. Then the traveler was eased, the main trimmed in, the backstays brought back and connected, and the staysail reset. After a final trim, we were done — until the next jibe. After a few days at sea, we'd banked enough practice that a six-person watch, plus Cam, could do it at night.

George Lewis, Cam's dad, started a ritual that we came to follow every evening. At the 1800 change of watch, we would sample three bottles of wine. George would note the name, year, and our opinions of the taste. Sometimes we'd get into a fourth bottle, but it left plenty to keep us going till landfall. We'd then stuff each bottle with a note offering a modest prize to anyone who found it and toss it overboard.

After a week, our days in the ocean took on an easy rhythm. On one typical day, we saw two ships, flew a kite, took bucket baths, and kept up regular maintenance and cleaning. As the wind came further after, we

Peter Johnstone throwing a message overboard

Preparing for the incoming squall

took to flying the Quad, a large downwind sail with two clews to give it more sail area. Tom Yale counted the steps to perform a jibe when we were flying the Quad — 17 individual procedures! — but it was pretty routine for us at this stage. *Team Adventure* was definitely not meant to be sailed with a small crew. You'd need at least six or seven if you did not have to stand watches. Cam did the last part of The Race with just nine from New Zealand to Marseilles. That's a pretty thin crew.

After two weeks at sea, we found ourselves about 850 miles east of the Bahamas with a 20-knot southeast breeze. We were smoking at 20-26 knots and sometimes more!

At one point, I said perhaps we should stop in Antigua since Antigua Race Week was happening at that time. We were heading that way, and for a while the discussions seemed to indicate it was a strong possibility. Cam was worried we would lose some of the crew to the party in Antigua and from the info on the weather forecast, he decided to go north and then west. We decided to stop in San Salvador instead to change some crew.

The forecast called for a frontal zone, which would send the wind all over the place, from light-and-variable to squally, so we knew we'd have to be on our toes. After we punched through it, the winds were predicted to go northeast and be quite strong for the following night and day before they eased off.

In spite of the strong wind and spray flying, the air was hot and sticky. Still, that was better than the reports of cold and snow we got from home. It was fun in that weather to be moving so fast, and it was especially fun to be at the helm. We began taking shorter hitches at the wheel: in those conditions, it takes a great deal of concentration to stay in the groove. When we came off the top of a wave and headed down, the whole boat would hum and the rudders would cavitate to add to the thrill.

The acceleration with this boat was awesome. Despite its massive size, its carbon fiber structure is very light. When the apparent wind moves forward, the boat actually jumps and tosses you back. With all the noise, the heat, and the jerking, you would think it was difficult to sleep. But we all got used to it.

On the early-morning dog watch of our last night before landfall, we saw a huge meteor. It lit up half the sky and broke into two pieces trailing smaller pieces behind it before ending in a bright green flash.

We rocketed to San Salvador at average speeds of about 25 knots in big swells and 20 to 30 knots of wind — over 500 miles in one 24-hour period.

We reached the north tip of the island on the evening of April 21, but with quite a bit of daylight ahead. After several tries, we made contact with a Club Med dive boat, which escorted us through the reef to a mooring buoy. They also gave us the use of their Zodiac inflatable boat with an outboard engine. This was great, since we were about a third of a mile offshore and had no dinghy.

The Zodiac was a little soft, and the engine looked questionable. But we soon had several groups going to shore, arriving extremely wet because of the chop behind the reef and the strong winds creating lots of spray and waves over the bow. We hiked to the Club Med Resort and were greeted by a guard at the entrance who had her rulebook out. It did not have a rule in it for visiting yachts and people hiking to the gate.

After 20 minutes and lots of phone calls, finally she let us in. As it turned out, Club Med gave us a complimentary dinner in their big dining area and buffet. For this first meal ashore we stuffed ourselves, drank copious amounts of wine, put the extra bottles in bags, and went to a local bar and disco near Cockburn Town to get a little flavor of the local scene.

The next day, the dive boat had taken back their Zodiac, but the hotel let us use a Boston Whaler. On the first trip in, the Club Med driver hit the reef several times and screwed up the prop, so they barely made it to dock. That was the end of the Boston Whaler for us. Cam tried to gather everyone on shore together for a ride to the airport, but it was like herding cats. Some were in the fishing village trying to borrow a Zodiac, some were still relaxing at the resort and nursing hangovers, and others were off sightseeing at the Columbus Monument.

The Bahamian customs official then called us into his area and wanted to know why we had not all checked in before. Cam explained that we'd tried, but couldn't find anyone. We had all of the passports, but he wanted to see everyone and get their signatures. The guys were fortunate to find a fishing boat at the marina to help get people in and out from the boat for the customs dilemma. Fortunately the plane arrived late. What a zoo!

With everyone on board by midafternoon, including four new crewmembers who'd flown in, we made preparations to go to sea. We had set a safety anchor out, and without a boat had no normal way of retrieving it. The wind was blowing over 30 knots, so motoring backwards (we were moored stern-to) was not going to work. So Hugh Piggins and Tom Gonzales donned scuba equipment, took a canvas bag with them, and tied it to the anchor 25 feet down, and then inflated it from their tanks, raising the anchor and chain. We were then able to pull in on a separate line they had attached. Impressive!

Right after this we got hit with a torrential downpour and strong gale winds, so we went into a half-hour holding pattern. We finally took off with a double

Dinner at Club Med with the crew

reef and the staysail in about 25-30 knots of wind. Just when we were settling in and setting the watches, we got hit with a gale-force blast of wind that had to be over 50 knots and rounded the boat up in a multiple g-force turn. Cam was at the helm and wrestled it down while we released the mainsheet, traveler, and staysail sheets. We then dropped the staysail and got the boat under control. With the wind still well over 30, we put a third reef in the main and sailed that way with no headsail until the two o'clock watch. The waves were really big, and our new crew wasn't yet acclimated: some were feeding the fish after all the rocking and rolling. The wind finally eased off a little in the dark morning hours, and changed to a more favorable direction. With things easing up, we took two reefs out and put up the Mule with the staysail. We made good speed to Savannah with sunny skies, clear blue water, medium-sized swells, and our bellies full from a good scrambled-egg breakfast Cam made at the 0600 watch change.

The trip was truly the experience of a lifetime, and I can't tell you how thankful our whole crew was to Cam and his partner Larry Rosenfeld for the invitation. We made new friends and sailed over 6,000 miles in one of the world's fastest boats. It can't get much better than that. In our last hours before Savannah, we shook out the final reef in the main so we could turn on the afterburners for the final run to the barn.

Team Adventure

Afterword

Toward the Windward Mark: Looking Ahead

OUR BUSINESS PHILOSOPHY

Peter and I have long believed there is a word that should apply to almost every action and decision. That word is honesty.

I got my first lesson in honesty shortly after we started the business — back when we were building those first six boats for Ohio State University. Like almost every boatbuilder, we were behind by quite a few weeks. When our customers called and wanted to know when we were going to deliver, I lied. I said they would be ready in about a week.

Peter overheard me and was furious. He made me call them back and tell them I was wrong, that we were further behind and would not be able to deliver for a few more weeks. This was very embarrassing, but it taught me a good lesson. For one thing, I didn't have to keep on lying each week. Taking the beating once is a lot easier than building one lie on top of another. It's not easy to do, and the customer is going to be angry or disappointed, but that's the end of it.

Common sense? You bet.

There are so many books put out by successful businessman and those who believe they know what it takes to succeed. I've often wondered which are correct, or if they are all right, or if they are just made up. Peter and I have read quite a few of them and have gleaned a bit of knowledge here and there. We don't remember what we read and what we created.

It was not until very recently that we actually wrote down the principles and goals of the company. This was done at the insistence of our young future company leaders, who felt it was important for us to clearly state our philosophy. As we were getting older, they were looking for the security and understanding of the legacy we wanted to preserve for future generations.

In 1999, we were looking for a fresh perspective in our advertising and marketing department. We hired a young sailor, Bill Goggins, who just finished his MBA at Marquette University. He had a lot of energy and enthusiasm for sailing and for Harken. In a few years, he had the department reorganized and running smoothly on new systems, not something we were focused on yet. When Peter and I decided to semi-retire in 2008, we decided he had the right kind of energy we needed and appointed him CEO of Harken USA. He got us involved in the project to state our corporate philosophy.

They termed this set of goals "The Weather Mark." This of course is usually the first upwind mark in a sailboat that sets the tone of the race. Reaching the weather mark in the front of the pack requires a number of factors including boat speed and choosing the right tack. The wind is constantly shifting and the velocity is changing so it is critical to choose the fastest direction to the mark. This analogy can be applied to almost any of the choices one has to make in life.

Harken's The Weather Mark is as follows, starting with a brief description of what we think we are as a business.

Harken, Inc. is the leading provider of sailboat hardware and accessories. We design, engineer, manufacture, and distribute cutting-edge and practical solutions for the global sailing community, and effective related industrial applications. We are focused on serving and providing the customer with the best products in the world.

Our company philosophy is based on the following goals.

- We focus on our customers and our market. Serving our customers with integrity is the most important thing we do.
- We focus on innovation. We search for the correct solutions to the performance problems of the sailing community and unique industrial requirements.
- We strive to bring solutions to the market quickly, but only when our solution is complete.

- We strive for the highest quality at the lowest reasonable price. If forced to choose between quality and price, we choose quality.
- We structure Harken so that all Harken staff are as close as possible to the customer.
- We empower and train our people to lead, manage, make decisions, be efficient, and serve our marketplace with integrity. Our greatest asset is our employees.
- We empower our people to think creatively and search for the best solutions.
- We operate Harken with a culture of mutual respect and teamwork among our customers, employees, distributors, suppliers, and industry professionals.
- We strive for a continuous increase in our financial strength.
- Our brand is non-negotiable and must have exactly the same meaning across the globe.
- Peter put it in a shorter version as follows:
- Keep the wellbeing of your people first!
- Make the best products at a fair price.
- Service your customer beyond their expectations.
- Never lose your sense of right from wrong, the basic judgment taught by your mother and father.

It can be very difficult for managers and owners to remember that our objectives include much more than making money. At Harken, we concluded that money is the byproduct of running a company well and with common sense.

Today we have over 400 people working at our two new factories in Limido Comasco, Italy, and Pewaukee, Wisconsin. Italy makes the winches, and we make all the other items in Pewaukee. The factories are custom-designed for "Lean Manufacturing Techniques" to maximize efficiency.

The company is managed by a team of folks who have been with us for over 10 years and understand the importance we place on our people — our most important asset. Peter and I have stepped back and let them do things their way. We had a seat-of-the-pants style, which worked well for us. But change had to come with the growth and size of the operation. We now have departments called IT and HR, which we just learned how to spell. The one area that we do still get involved with are issues dealing with our senior managers. Financial information and corporate direction are board decisions. Peter and I are cochairmen of the board, which is their nice way of telling us to butt out. The team is great, and the company is in good hands.

Risk is critical to growth, and we take our share. How much we are willing to gamble is based on our knowledge of the industry, the economic outlook, currency rates and our relationship with our bank. We then go to a bar and make the final decision over a couple of beers. Usually, it comes to one question: If everything went bad, could we survive?

We purchased Accurate Products, the company that had been making most of our hardware since we started, and with it came an enormous amount of CNC milling machines, lathes, and tools — plus lots of nonmarine industrial accounts, and the diversification made it more attractive. In addition the economy had gone into a serious depression and the price was right. Before buying Accurate we needed a much bigger building, so the wait was perfect since building contractors were hungry for business, and we needed more space than we could have anticipated before the purchase. We found that we could save more than a million dollars if we had the cash. With a new factory in Italy, a new one in Pewaukee, and the purchase of Accurate Products we had over 30 million dollars invested. But with the help of the bank we did the deed and so far the gain in efficiency of being under one roof has been encouraging.

THE FUTURE

The direction of the Harken company is quite clear. We will remain the best of class in the sailing industry and increase diversification in products and manufacturing to grow and protect ourselves against the swings in the economy.

So where do we go from here? Who knows? As Peter says, "Blunder Forth."

Parkinson's Disease has slowed me down and is a new challenge. But with the support of my family and friends and a never-ending supply of memories, I can only say: "It's been a hoot!"

Harken USA state-of-the-art, 173,000-square-foot facility in Pewaukee, Wisconsin

Harken USA CNC machine area

Large-part CNC machine

Injection-molding machine area

Harken Italy state-of-the-art, 86,000-square-foot building in Limido Comasco

Harken Italy winch assembly area

Testing area

Assembly robot